PENGUIN BOOKS

ESSENTIAL ARABIC

Also published in this series:

Essential Chinese (Mandarin)
Essential Japanese

ESSENTIAL ARABIC

A Guidebook to Language and Culture

COMPILED BY LEXUS
*with Alex Chapman
and Ashraf Ghali*

PENGUIN BOOKS

PENGUIN BOOKS

Published by the Penguin Group
27 Wrights Lane, London W8 5TZ, England
Viking Penguin Inc., 40 West 23rd Street, New York, New York 10010, USA
Penguin Books Australia Ltd, Ringwood, Victoria, Australia
Penguin Books Canada Ltd, 2801 John Street, Markham, Ontario, Canada L3R 1B4
Penguin Books (NZ) Ltd, 182–190 Wairau Road, Auckland 10, New Zealand

Penguin Books Ltd, Registered Offices: Harmondsworth, Middlesex, England

First published 1990
10 9 8 7 6 5 4 3 2 1

Filmset in Linotron Plantin Light
Made and printed in Great Britain by
Cox & Wyman Ltd, Reading

CONTENTS

Shouf!
= Look!

INTRODUCTION

This is a guidebook to Arabic language and culture. Information is presented in one single A–Z listing in which dictionary and phrasebook elements are interwoven with descriptive passages on language, grammar and culture.

The dictionary/phrasebook elements give a vocabulary of some 1,500 everyday words and expressions, providing an excellent basis for self-expression in the foreign language.

The Arabic words and expressions are presented using the Roman alphabet. A pronunciation guide has been added so that the Arabic words and expressions can easily be read out (see also the notes on pronunciation on page ix).

The language and grammar notes provide explanations of how the Arabic language works. If you want to go a little further, these sections will enable you to develop some basic skills with the Arabic language and to develop a knowledge of its structure.

More language notes and some useful expressions are given within the culture note entries: typical polite expressions, what to say in specific circumstances, how to address people etc. – all valuable language tips for the traveller.

The culture notes and cross-cultural comparisons cover a wide range of topics – from Ramadan to marriage, from eating to clothing, from the calendar to cushions – all having the same purpose of acting as a guide to a number of countries that are not just foreign but different.

And this is an important point to remember: whereas a book on, say, Italian, can deal with one country, a book on Arabic has a total of no less than nineteen separate countries to deal with. We have tried to indicate some of the differences between the various countries of the Arabic world as well as pointing to features which they have in common.

This book can operate at various levels. You can use it as a kind of travel book, to be read at home; you can take it abroad with you and use it as a dictionary/ phrasebook; you can use it as an introduction to the Arabic language; or you can simply dip into it as a source of information about another civilization.

NOTE

For nouns which have irregular plurals the plural form is given in square brackets after the translation. Regulars can be formed by following the rules set out under PLURALS.

For an explanation of the second verb form given in square brackets after each verb translation (e.g. bàda' [yàbda']) see the entry on VERBS.

NOTES ON PRONUNCIATION

For more detailed comments on the pronunciation of Arabic see the entry PRONUNCIATION. The following points will help you read the translations in this book which have been written by transferring the Arabic sounds to the Roman alphabet:

Vowels

a, ah	as in 'sad'
aa	as in 'tar'
ai	as in 'Cairo'
ay	as in 'pay'
e	as in 'red'
ee	as in 'green'
i	as in 'fit'
o	as in 'top'
oo	as in 'food'
ou	as in 'loud'
u	as in 'look'

Consonants

The six letters given in small capitals – A, D, H, S, T and Z – are pronounced more forcefully than their lower-case equivalents; pronounce them with a short expulsion of air.

gh	is like a French 'r', coming from the back of the throat
kh	is like the 'ch' in the Scottish pronunciation of 'loch'
j	as in 'Jimmy' (in Egypt a hard 'g')
q	is a 'k' sound coming from the back of the mouth
th	as in 'thick'

When a vowel or the first of a pair of vowels has an accent, this means that that part of the word should be stressed.

The apostrophe in translations indicates what is called a 'hamza'. This sounds like a short catch in the breath.

x

Final	Median	Initial	Isolated	
ا	ا	ا–أ	أ	a
ب	ﺒ	ﺑ	ب	b
ت	ﺘ	ﺗ	ت	t
ث	ﺜ	ﺛ	ث	th
ج	ﺠ	ﺟ	ج	j
ح	ﺤ	ﺣ	ح	H
خ	ﺨ	ﺧ	خ	kh
ﺪ	ﺪ	د	د	d
ﺬ	ﺬ	ذ	ذ	z
ر	ر	ر	ر	r
ز	ز	ز	ز	z
س	ﺴ	ﺳ	س	s
ش	ﺸ	ﺷ	ش	sh
ص	ﺼ	ﺻ	ص	S
ض	ﻀ	ﺿ	ض	D
ط	ﻄ	ﻃ	ط	T
ظ	ﻈ	ﻇ	ظ	Z
ع	ﻌ	ﻋ	ع	A
غ	ﻐ	ﻏ	غ	gh
ف	ﻔ	ﻓ	ف	f
ق	ﻘ	ﻗ	ق	q
ك	ﻜ	ﻛ	ك	k
ل	ﻠ	ﻟ	ل	l
م	ﻤ	ﻣ	م	m
ن	ﻨ	ﻧ	ن	n
و	و	و	و	w
ﺔ	ﻬ	ﻫ	ة	h
ى	ﻴ	ﻳ	ى	y
ڤ	ﻔ	ﻓ	ڤ	v
چ	ﭽ	ﭼ	چ	SH

A

a, an
There is no word for 'a' in Arabic, no indefinite article. So to say, for example, 'a book' or 'a car' you must simply say:

kitàab book
sayàarah car

If, for example, you want to rent a car, you would say:

urèed astà'jir sayàarah

which means literally:

I want to rent car

The word 'a' is, as you can see, redundant.

about (*approximately*) Hawàalee
about four o'clock Hawàalee as-sàa'ah arbà'ah

above (*preposition*) fouq

accident (*traffic etc.*) Hàadith

adaptor (*for voltage changes*) moowàjih

address Aunwàan
what's the address? aysh al-Aunwàan?
could you write the address down? mùmkin tàktub al-Aunwàan?

ADDRESSES
Addresses must be written either entirely in Arabic or entirely in Roman script. It is not acceptable to mix Roman and Arabic letters or numerals in the same address. To get round this difficulty most businessmen who travel in the Arab world have business cards with their details in Roman script on one side and Arabic on the other. Their Arab counterparts will have the same sort of cards and any embarrassment is avoided.

Arab postal workers can cope with addresses written in Roman script, even if this means delay. Write the address exactly as you would in Britain and underline the town or city. As a matter of interest, addresses written in Arabic are written completely 'upside-down' compared with the British pattern, with the country at the top, then the city and address below and finally the name of the addressee at the very bottom.

ADDRESSING PEOPLE

If you do not know the person you are addressing at all you would simply address him or her as

yaa ustàaz
sir

or

yaa sayìdah
madam

without using an actual name at all.

The moment you are acquainted you exchange first names and use them from that point onward. You might be addressed as

yaa David

or

yaa Peter

and you would address your colleague as

yaa Mustafa

or

yaa Ahmed

To this form of address is often added

akhèe
my brother

sadèeqee
my friend

or very affectionately

Habèebee
my loved one

For example:

yaa Mustàfa akhèe
hi, Mustafa old chap

Surnames, which are all-important in the West, are used in the Arab world only to differentiate between various people called, for example, Ahmed. It is not over-familiar to use first names from the moment of meeting.

The word **yaa** is usually prefixed to the name or title.

When addressing people of very high rank, such as ministers or ambassadors etc., you would use

yaa ustàaz

at the opening and stay with this without using a personal name until you know him 'personally' –

that is until he invites you out, introduces you to his non-business friends or to members of his family. You would then move to

yaa ustàaz Ahmed

until you felt he was an equal and then revert to the normal form among equals:

yaa Ahmed

The title Doctor (**doktòor**) is very rare and prestigious, because there are very few Arab universities where the degree can be obtained, and the title is used for both medical and academic doctors. You use it as you would use **ustàaz** (see above); later with the man's first name: **yaa doktòor!** or **yaa doktòor Muhammad!**

Because the title is so much rarer than it is in the West the holder of such a title uses it everywhere as a status symbol. In fact it is hard to imagine any Arab not using an honorific he was entitled to.

When addressing an elderly man whose name is Ahmed it is customary to call him:

Haaj Ahmed

Haaj is really the title given to people who have made the pilgrimage to Mecca, but it is used generally for the elderly as a term of respect.

ADJECTIVES

Unlike English, adjectives in Arabic are placed after the noun they describe. They must agree with that noun, masculine or feminine and singular or plural. If the adjective is definite – has 'the' before it – so does the adjective.

Indefinite

a book (*masc.*)
kitàab

a big book
kitàab kabèer

a time (*masc.*)
waqt

a long time
waqt Tawèel

a car (*fem.*)
sayàarah

a small car
sayàarah Saghèerah

a room (*fem.*)
ghùrfah

a warm room
ghùrfah daafèe'ah

So far so good. There is just one extra point to remember, although many Arabs speaking quickly will ignore it: if a masculine indefinite noun, such as the first two examples above, is the object of a sentence, it and any adjectives attached to it take an object suffix **-an**. Whether you pronounce this suffix **-an** is optional. Similarly you will hear it from some Arabic speakers, especially educated ones, and not from others.

Here are the above examples as objects of a sentence:

I bought a big book
ishtaràytu kitàab(an) kabèer(an)

we spent a long time there
ìHna qaDàyna wàqt(an) Tawèel(an) hunàak

The feminine is not affected by this:

I bought a small car
àna ishtaràytu sayàarah Saghèerah

we asked them for a warm room
Talàbna mìnhum ghùrfah daafèe'ah

Indefinite plural
The golden rule is: all human/plural nouns take a plural adjective, masculine or feminine, as you would expect, *but* all non-human plural nouns take a *feminine singular* adjective, whether they are masculine or feminine themselves. Feminine plural adjectives are formed by removing the **-ah** ending from the adjective and adding **-àat**. This **-àat** ending always carries the stress. So here are some humans with their plural adjective:

rich men
rijàal aghniyàa

happy fools
majaanèen su'adàa

trained nurses
mumariDàat muDarabàat

beautiful ladies
sayidàat jameelàat

And some non-humans with their feminine singular adjective:

> **spacious houses** (*masc.*)
> bùyut waasì'ah

> **big hotels** (*masc.*)
> fanàadiq kabèerah

> **cheap cars** (*fem.*)
> sayaaràat rakhèesah

> **busy towns** (*fem.*)
> mùdun muzdaHìmah

Definite singular

When a noun is definite its adjective becomes definite as well (*see also* THE). Otherwise the rules are just the same as for the indefinite.

> **the man**
> ar-ràjul

> **the clever man**
> ar-ràjul ash-shàaTir

> **the manageress**
> al-mudèerah

> **the young manageress**
> al-mudèerah aS-Saghèerah

> **the blue shirt**
> al-qamèes al-àzraq

> **the huge school**
> al-madràsah aD-Dàkhmah

Definite plural

Human:

> **the small boys**
> al-awlàad aS-Sighàar

> **the clever professors**
> al-asaatèezah al-azkiyàa

> **the angry teachers** (*fem.*)
> al-mudarisàat al-ghuDbaanàat

> **the busy ladies**
> as-sayidàat al-mashghoolàat

And non-human:

> **the heavy books** (*masc.*)
> al-kùtub ath-thaqèelah

> **the china cups** (*masc.*)
> al-fanàajin aS-Seenèe

> **the cheap cars** (*fem.*)
> as-sayaaràat ar-rakhèesah

the expensive tickets (*fem.*)
at-tazàakir al-ghaalèeyah

In Arabic, adjectives are often used on their own as nouns, taking the masculine or feminine endings as appropriate:

the beautiful (woman)
al-jamèelah

the small (one)
as-saghèer

advance: in advance muqàdaman
advance payment dùf'ah muqàdamah

ADVERBS

The normal way of forming an adverb is to add the ending -(y)an to the relevant adjective. For example:

quick	sarèeʌ
quickly	sarèe'an
slow	baтèe'
slowly	baтèe'an
temporary	muwàqat
temporarily	muwàqatan
final	akhèer
finally	akhèeran
financial	màalee
financially	màaleeyan
basic	asàas
basically	asàasan

Unlike English, where it can be considered uneducated to use an adjective instead of an adverb, Arabic adjectives are often used instead of adverbs in everyday speech. For example:

he stayed in my house temporarily
hùwa sàkan fee bàytee muwàqatan

and finally he travelled from Riyadh by plane
wa akhèeran hùwa sàafar min ar-rìyaD biт-Tayàarah

advertisement iʌlàan

aeroplane тayàarah

after (*preposition*) ba'd
after lunch ba'd al-ghazàa'
after you! tafàDal!

You will hear this last expression used very often in the Arab world. Age before beauty is the rule, and guests precede everyone regardless of attractiveness! Women are never met socially in the Peninsula, but elsewhere, where they are more emancipated, they walk with their husband or chaperon and among educated Arabs, and in the big cities 'ladies first' is the rule, as it usually is in the West.

afternoon ba'd az-zùhr
   this afternoon al-youm ba'd az-zùhr
   in the afternoon ba'd az-zùhr
   good afternoon as-salàam Alàykum

   As-salàam Alàykum, which means literally 'peace (be) upon you', is the equivalent of the French *bonjour* and is the standard greeting given at any time of day. There is, as in French, no special phrase meaning 'good afternoon'.

aftershave koolòoniyaa

afterwards ba'dàyn

again màrah thaanèeyah

against Did
   I'm against the idea àna moosh moowàafiq

agent (*in business*) wakèel

ago: a year ago min sànah
   two months ago min shahràyn
   that was a long time ago hàaza min mùdah Tawèelah

agree: I agree àna moowàafiq
   do you agree? ànta moowàafiq?
   I don't agree àna moosh moowàafiq

agreement (*contract*) itifàaq
   (*document*) Aqd

AGREEMENT

There are two areas of Arabic grammar where agreement must be made: between the noun and any adjective it may have and between a subject and its verb. Let us look at the noun and adjective agreement first.

Adjectives follow the noun they qualify and must agree with that noun in gender and 'definiteness' – the definite article goes with the article as well as with the noun:

   a rich man
   ràjul ghanèe

the rich man
ar-ràjul al-ghanèe

a rich woman
sayìdah ghanèeyah

the rich woman
as-sayìdah al-ghanèeyah

cold coffee
qàhwah baarìdah

the cold coffee
al-qàhwah al-baarìdah

Plural nouns which are human must, of course, take plural adjectives masculine or feminine as appropriate:

small boys
awlàad sighàar

the small boys
al-awlàad aS-sighàar

pretty girls
banàat jameelàat

the pretty girls
al-banàat al-jameelàat

famous men
rijàal mashàahir

the famous men
ar-rijàal al-mashàahir

Plural nouns which are not human are, illogically, grammatically feminine singular regardless of whether they are normally masculine or feminine.

cheap books (*masc.*)
kùtub rakhèesah

the cheap books
al-kùtub ar-rakhèesah

clean cars (*fem.*)
sayaaràat naZèefah

the clean cars
as-sayaaràat an-naZèefah

crowded markets (*fem.*)
aswàaq muzdaHìmah

the crowded markets
al-aswàaq al-muzdaHìmah

Agreement between a subject and its verb comes naturally to us in English: 'I go' but 'it goes' – 'you swim' but 'she swims'. In Arabic the same principle of the verb changing with the subject is taken a step further – every person, 'I', 'you', 'she', 'we' etc. has a special form of the verb to go with it. This means of course that the personal pronouns do not *need* to be used with any verb, since the verb already tells us what the subject must be.

For example, in the past tense any verb associated with 'we' (ìнna) ends in its own special ending of **-na**. For example:

katàbna
we wrote

The pronoun need only be added for emphasis:

not he but we bought it!
moo hùwa inàma ìнna ishtaraiynàha!

See also ADJECTIVES, VERBS

air hawàa'

air-conditioning takyèef

AIR-CONDITIONING
Air-conditioning is used in very many Arab buildings and it is true to say that no new buildings of any size at all which have rooms to be lived or worked in are constructed without air-conditioning being the main fixture. Apart from offices, shops, hotels and schools, nowadays in all the wealthy Arab countries even the taxis are air-conditioned.

Away from the big cities houses tend to be fitted with non-electric air-conditioning. Windows have an extra shutter made of net and containing a layer of reeds and rushes which is pulled to during the hot part of the day. A thin hose runs along the top of the shutter dripping water down through the rushes. The cooling and moisturizing effect is every bit as good as the electric version, but it is silent and costs almost nothing to run.

airline shìrkat Taiyràan
   which airline is it? ay shìrkat Taiyràan?

airmail barèed jòuwee

airport maтàar مطار

   to the airport please lil-maтàar lou samàнt

alcohol
   Two words can be used for 'alcohol': **khamr** means 'wine' and **muskiràat** means 'intoxicants' of all kinds.

ALCOHOL

The consumption of alcohol is theoretically forbidden in Islam but each country enforces this prohibition to a different extent.

Many of the Arabian Peninsula states, particularly Saudi Arabia, forbid any consumption of alcohol whatsoever. In Saudi Arabia it is forbidden even to be in possession of alcohol and there are very strict penalties indeed for breaking this prohibition, such as public whipping and imprisonment. Summary deportation is the best to be hoped for.

In many of the Mediterranean Arab states, however, attitudes are more relaxed. But although alcoholic drinks are usually available in big hotels in, for example, Egypt, Syria and Lebanon, they may be hard to find elsewhere. Availability also depends on the size and religious environment of the city you are in. Really the best advice that can be offered to a Westerner travelling anywhere in the Peninsula at least is to use the visit as an opportunity to give the liver a rest and take a renewed interest in the enormous variety of fruit juices and soft drinks which are available everywhere in the Arab world.

Westerners often view the prohibition or disapproval of alcohol consumption as in some way restricting human choice and freedom, imagining that every Arab is secretly longing to try the forbidden fruit in an attempt to improve his often humdrum life. Nothing could be further from the truth. Most Muslims do not drink because it runs counter to the whole tenor of Muslim teaching and philosophy. This holds that the only faculty separating man from the animals is his reason and so anything which de-humanizes man by clouding that reason has to be resisted. They take the view that, by drinking to excess, man becomes temporarily no better than a beast and loses the respect humans are entitled to. Perhaps this explains the basic contempt with which many Arabs view hard-drinking Westerners.

Algeria al-jazàa'ir

Algerian (*noun, adjective*) jazàa'iree

Algiers al-jazàa'ir

all kul
    all the rooms kul al-ghùruf

all my money kul fulòosee
that's all, thanks bas, shùkran

all right tamàam
is that all right? hal hàaza tamàam?
that's all right tamàam

Allah àllah
praise be to Allah al-Hàmdu lìllah

almost taqrèeban

alone li-wàHdee
I'm travelling alone àna musàafir li-wàHdee

ALPHABET

The Arabic alphabet consists of twenty-nine letters which are written from right to left. There are no capital letters. Each letter has up to four different forms: one when it stands alone, one at the beginning of a word, one in the middle of a word and one when it is the final letter. The letters are strung together just like our Roman letters are in handwriting. The dots are crucially important to the legibility of a word. For example, **b** is ب. In a sense **b** is just a dot below a line, any line. The line in this letter is just a line to put a dot under to show you where the dot is! **n** is one dot above a line, **t** is two dots above a line and **th** is three dots above; and so on. You can see the others by looking at the table on p. x.

When an Arab reads a word he basically looks at the dots, not the line of the word. You can imagine now that even a speck on the paper near a word that could be a dot can render the word incomprehensible, at least at first glance.

It will be noticed from the above table that the alphabet seems to consist almost entirely of consonants. This is in fact true, for Arabic words do not contain written short vowels (although the long vowels are written). The reader is faced with a string of consonants but knows from experience how the vowels must be added to make the word make sense. Obviously the same written word can often be pronounced in more than one way, but usually only one version makes sense in the context. If there is serious ambiguity, extra marks are added to show what the vowels are, but this is only very rarely done. The most frequent use of these extra dots you will encounter is in the names of foreign products. Clearly, if the product is new and Arabs have never seen the name before they often cannot pronounce it properly – hence the need for extra help.

The Arabic alphabet is not therefore phonetic in the Western sense. Because the vowels are not written it is impossible to 'say' any written word with much conviction without knowing exactly where to put the vowels. In a nutshell, a reader of Arabic needs a vast vocabulary, since he has to know every word before he can read it! In practice a lot of educated guesses have to be made using the pattern of the consonants to assume where the vowels should be.

already min qabl

also kamàan

although mà'an

altogether bil-kàamil
  what does that make altogether? shoo al-majmòoʌ?

always dàa'iman

am *see* be

America amirèeka   أمريكا

American (*adjective*) amirèekee
  she's/he's **American** hùwa amirèekee/hìya amiree-kèeya
  the **Americans** al-amireekàan

and wa

another thàanee
  another tea, please shaay thàanee lou samàнt
  another cup of coffee finjàan qàhwah thàanee
  I'd like another room (*a different one*) àna urèed ghùrfah mukhtàlifah

answer (*noun*) ijàabah
  there was no answer (*on telephone*) at-tilifòon maa yarùd

any ay
  have you any English books? ʌ̀ndak ay kùtub inglizèeyah?
  have you got any change? ʌ̀ndak ay fàkah?

When English uses 'any' emphatically as in the sense of 'haven't you got any at all?' Arabic just uses the

tone of voice to convey the emphasis and you
actually say (in an aggrieved tone):

> **haven't you got some of them?**
> làysa Àndak mìnhum?

anyone ay shakhs

anything ay shay

apology iАtizàar
please accept our apologies àrjook taqàbal iАtizàarna

approximately taqrèeban

April ibrèel

Arab (*noun, adjective*) Àrabee

Arab league al-jàami'at ad dowal al-Arabèeyah

Arabic (*adjective*) Àrabee
(*language*) al-Arabèeyah

ARABIC

As the Arabic language developed in its written form
from the seventh century A D so did the different
forms of writing it: the art of calligraphy.

Since Islam prohibits the depiction of images,
portraits and sculpture, much creative artistic energy
was spent in developing calligraphy as one of the
major art forms. At an early date two separate styles
of calligraphy evolved: **Kufic** and **Nashki**.

The hallmark of **Kufic** script is its angularity and
pattern and it became the style chiefly used in
calligraphic art, together with the **Thuluth** script
which was drawn using a whole variety of shapes
and designs.

All the examples that follow say the same thing:

> **In the Name of Allah the Merciful the Compas-
> sionate**
> bism ìllah ar-raНmàn ar-raНèem

which is the opening verse of the Koran. The Kufic
and Thuluth versions are:

بسم الله الرحمن الرحيم

بِسْمِ اللَّهِ الرَّحْمَنِ الرَّحِيمِ

The other main script, **Nashki**, is more easily
legible and was the script more often used for
copying manuscripts and documents. Nowadays it is

the main script used in newspapers, in magazines
and on typewriters:

بسم الله الرحمن الرحيم

There is another kind of script which you may see
in newspapers and which is often used for headlines:
Ruq'ah. This has a nice handwritten look to it and,
as you can see, the set of two dots is joined into one
stroke – as they are in handwriting:

بسم الله الرحمن الرحيم

See also ALPHABET, LANGUAGE, WRITING.

are *see* be

arm ziràa'

arrivals (*airport sign*) wusòol

arrive wàsal [yàsil]
he's arriving tomorrow ba-yàsil bùkra

ARTICLES *see* **a, the**

ashtray Tafàayah

ask sà'al [yàs'al]
I'll ask him àna sa-'as'àlhu
could you ask him? mùmkin tas'àlhu?

asleep nàayim
he's still asleep lissàhu nàayim

assistant: my assistant musaa'ìdee

at fee
at my hotel fee fundùqee
at the airport feel-maTàar
at 9 o'clock as-sà'ah tìs'ah

August aghùsTus

aunt àmmah

Australia ustraalèeyaa   استراليا

Australian (*adjective*) ustràalee
he's/she's Australian hùwa ustràalee/hìya ustraa-
lèeyah
the Australians al-ustraaleeyèen

autumn al-kharèef
in the autumn feel-kharèef

average mutawàsiT
on average feel-mutawàsiT

B

back (*of body*) zahr
   my back zàhree
   I'll be right back sa'àrja' Hàalan
   when we go back home làmaa nàrja' balàdna
   back home in England fee ingiltìra balàdee

bad (*person, food, deal*) moo zàyin

bag (*carrier-bag*) shànTah [(*pl*) shùnuT]
   (*suitcase*) shànTat sàfar

baggage shùnuT as-sàfar
   Bahrain al-baHràyn

ball-point pen qàlam jaaf

bank bank [(*pl*) bunòok] بنك

BANK
Banking hours vary greatly from country to country, but in general follow the pattern of banks in the West. But they do close at lunch-time. Banks are closed all day Friday and open on Sundays.

bank account Hisàab feel-bànk

bank loan sùlfah min al-bànk

bankrupt mùflis

bar (*drinks*) baar

bath bàaniyoo

bathroom Hamàam

BATHS
Baths are increasingly common in the Arab world, although most older houses have a shower room for washing.

battery baTaarèeyah

be
In Arabic there is no present tense of the verb 'to be' that we use so often in various forms in English: 'I am . . .'; 'you are . . .' etc. So, for example, instead of saying:

   he is poor

you simply say:

> **he poor**
> hùwa faqèer

Similarly, for:

> I am tired

you say:

> **I tired**
> àna ta'abàan

A woman would of course use the feminine form of the adjective:

> **I am English**

would be:

> àna inglizèeyah

In the past tense the following forms are used (*see also* PAST TENSE):

I was	kùntu
you were (*to a man*)	kùnta
(*to a woman*)	kùnti
he, she, it was	kaan/kàanat
(*masc./fem.*)	
we were	kùna
you were (*plural*)	kùntum
they were (*people only*)	kàanoo

For example:

> **I was late**
> (àna) kùntu muta'àkhar

> **she was asleep**
> (hìya) kàanat naayìmah

The pronouns 'he', 'I' etc. are optional and are mainly used for emphasis. *See* PRONOUNS.

In the future tense the following forms are used (*see also* FUTURE TENSE):

I shall be	sa-àkoon
you will be (*masc.*)	sa-tàkoon
(*fem.*)	sa-takòonee
he, it will be (*masc.*)	sa-yàkoon
she will be	sa-tàkoon
we shall be	sa-nàkoon
you will be (*plural*)	sa-takòonoo
they will be (*people*)	sa-yakòonoo

Note that 'you will be' (*masc.*) is the same word as 'she will be'. This is an occasion where you might want to use the optional pronouns for clarity.

she will be
hìya sa-tàkoon

you (*masc.*) **will be**
ànta sa-tàkoon

Some examples of the future of 'to be' in use:

we shall be late
(ìHna) sa-nàkoon muta'akharèen

I shall be here
(àna) sa-àkoon hùna

Since all non-human plurals are grammatically feminine singular you use **hìya** for 'they' (*things*):

where are the plates?
wayn al-aTbàaq?

they are on the table
hìya AlaT-Tàawalah

beard zàqan

beautiful (*woman, day, meal*) jamèel

because mishàan
Note that **mishàan** really means 'by reason of . . .' and is followed by a noun. So:

I am here because I'm going to offer you a good deal
àna hùna mishàan àariD alàyk sàfqah mumtàazah

which literally means:

I am here by reason of offering you a good deal

bed sarèer [(*pl*) sarà'ir]
I have to go to bed làazim aròoH anàam
he's in bed hùwa nàayim

bedroom ghùrfat noum

BEDS
These days just about every Arab house has a bedroom, if not two or three. These are just the same as they are in the West and are a direct import which has become the norm since 1945. If only one of the rooms in a house is air-conditioned it will be the bedroom. However, many Arabs will tell you that sleeping in an air-conditioned bedroom gives them a streaming cold all summer and that they prefer to

take the mattress off the bed, take it out of the
bedroom altogether and put it down in the garden
and sleep underneath the stars – which is fine if you
regularly rise with the sun. Don't be surprised to
find some Arabs preferring the traditional way of
sleeping on mattresses – which they will keep rolled
up in the corner of the room during the daytime.

beef laHm al-bàqar

beer bèerah
    two beers, please zujaajatàyn bèerah lou samàHt

before qabl
    before the next meeting qabl al-ijtimàa' al-jàay
    haven't we met before? hal taqabàlna min qabl?

begin bàda' [yàbda']

behind khalf
    behind schedule muta'akharèen

BELCHING
There is a common and utterly erroneous belief,
which is presumably a relic of colonial attitudes, that
it is in some way good manners and polite in the
Arab world to belch, and even break wind, after a
meal. This is, so goes the myth, a sign of satisfaction
and appreciation and one's host will be honoured. In
the Arab world nothing could be considered more
vulgar or gross than to do either deliberately at any
time during a meal. If you must belch or break wind,
try and make it look accidental or do it in private!

believe sàdaq [yusàdiq]
    he'll never believe it mustaHèel yusadìqhaa

belly-dancer raqàasah

below (*spatially*) taHt
    (*less than*) àqal min . . .

best àHsan
    our best model moodèelna al-àHsan
    the best engineers àHsan al-muhandisèen
    we'll do our best sa-nàbzal qusàaree jùhdna

better àfDal
    that's better hàaza àfDal

between bayn

bid (*noun*) ATàa [(*pl*) ATèeyah]

big kabèer

bil¹ faatòorah [(*pl*) fawàatir]
 can I have the bill, please? mùmkin al-faatòorah lou samàнt?

bill of exchange kambeeyàalah

BILLS

The bill is always paid by the person who has invited the guests to eat or drink etc. Just occasionally, among a group of friends, it may fall to the person whose house is nearest to the venue, as he could be thought to be entertaining 'at home'. If you are entertaining Arab guests you will be expected to pay for everything. A good way of avoiding a public display of paying, which can embarrass Arab guests who may feel they really ought to pay when you are in their country, is to arrange with your hotel to put everything on your room bill. Even the most sensitive soul could not feel awkward about you signing a chit of paper at the end of the meal. Say:

 Dèefha àla нisàab ghurfàtee
 put it on my room number

It should be said that Arab custom requires everybody to make protestations about wanting to pay at the end of a meal but everybody knows in advance who will win this ritual battle – in fact there would be consternation if the host allowed anyone else to pay anything at all!

birthday Aèed meelàad
 happy birthday Aèed meelàad sa'èed

birthday card biтàaqat Aèed meelàad

BIRTHDAYS

Birthdays are celebrated in the Arab world just as they are in the West: with cakes, presents and much back-slapping – but no alcohol. As with all parties birthday celebrations are sex-segregated. So if a man throws a birthday-party for his wife, the wife will do all the cooking and have a party with the women while the man will have a separate party with the husbands of the women guests. Those men won't even see the birthday-girl! Birthday-cards are very common. Since Arab families are generally large, if you stay with an Arab family for more than a week or so you are sure to be invited to a birthday party somewhere.

biscuit baskwèet

bit qìT'ah
    a little bit qìT'ah saghèerah
    a bit better àHsan qalèelan
    a bit of chocolate qìT'at shokoolàatah

black àswad

blanket baTaanèeyah

bless you (*after sneeze*) yarHamàkum àllah (*literally: may Allah have mercy on you*)

blood dam

blood group fasèelat ad-dàm

blue àzraq

board of directors màjlis al-idàarah

boat safèenah [(*pl*) sùfun]
    by boat bis-safèenah

body jìsim

boiled egg bàyDah maslòoqah

book (*noun*) kitàab [(*pl*) kùtub]

borrow istàlaf [yastàlif]

boss ar-ra'èes
    my boss ra'èesee

both al-ithnàyn
    both of them hùmaa al-ithnàyn

bottle zujàajah

bottle-opener fatàaHah

bottom (*of box etc.*) qaa'

box sùndooq [(*pl*) sanàadiq]

boy wàlad [(*pl*) awlàad]

bra sootyàan

brake (*noun*) bràyk

branch (*of company*) fàra'

brand image inTibàa' as-sìnf

brandy bràandee

breach: a breach of contract ikhlàal bil-Àqd

bread khubz خبز

could I have some bread please? mùmkin tajèeb lee khubz lou samàнt?

BREAD
Bread to an Arab means unleavened bread; what we call 'pitta bread'.

breakfast fiтòor

BREAKFAST
Breakfast as taken in the Arab world is a substantial meal since it must last the eater through the whole morning's work – often the work of the day – until lunch at 2–3 p.m. It consists of a range of different dishes all laid out on the breakfast 'table' – very often a rug and cloth on the floor. It will include: beans (haricot), hard-boiled eggs, hard white salty cheese and fresh vegetables such as tomatoes, cucumber and grated carrot. The normal drink is tea, not coffee, and fruit juices and milk. This breakfast is usually eaten any time from 6 a.m. onwards, depending on the routine of the household.

bridge jìsir

briefcase shànтat awràaq

bring jaab [yajèeb]
I didn't bring it with me maa jibìtuhaa mà'ee

Britain breeтaanèeya بريطانيا

British breeтàanee
I'm British (*said by man*) àna breeтàanee
(*said by woman*) àna breeтaanèeyah

brochure kutàyib
our company brochure kutàyib shirkàtna

broken (*arm*) maksòorah
(*calculator*) mukhtàrib

brother akh

brown bùnee

budget (*noun*) meezaanèeyah

building (*edifice*) màbna [(*pl*) mabàanee]
(*construction work*) inshàa'

bus baas
 by bus bil-bàas

bus station maHàтat baasàat

bus stop mòuqif baasàat   موقف باص

business (*company*) shìrkah
 (*the act of trading*) shughl
 I'm here on business àna Àndee shughl hùna
 it's a pleasure to do business with you yashràfnee
 ata'àamul mà'ak
 we look forward to a fruitful business relationship
 ìnshaa àllah tàkoon Alàaqat Àmal muṭhmìrah
 business is business! ash-shùghl shughl!

BUSINESS

Contrary to popular belief, most business dealings
with Arabs are not the lengthy, Byzantine and
conspiratorial affairs of *The Thousand and One
Nights* – in fact since the Second World War, and
especially since the quadrupling of oil prices in 1973
and the resultant amassing of wealth by some Arab
states, an experienced élite of businessmen has
emerged in almost every country which effectively
runs the foreign trade affairs of their country. As a
foreign businessman the Westerner will invariably
find himself dealing with one of this élite. They may
wear traditional robes and probably will not drink,
but in most cases they are as canny and sophisticated
as any of their Western counterparts. In short, then,
a Westerner should not feel as if he is entering the
lion's den on a business visit to the Arab world and
should behave as he would on a business trip in the
West. But you should remember that there will be
little or no alcoholic drink around to relax you
through your business dealings.

This last point is important to consider as the
'style' of many Western businessmen includes a lot
of drinking and socializing while working. The
Westerner may find that his normal affable and
persuasive self becomes very ragged after a week of
pineapple-juice (although in Egypt and Lebanon
this will not apply so much).

Arab businessmen do not much care for very
'straight talking' along the lines of 'well, if push
comes to shove . . .' and 'well, of course we have the
whip-hand . . .' and so on, so favoured by the

Americans. Make them feel they really have a choice, and fill your conversations with plenty of admiration – but not sycophancy. Objects of admiration can include the man's character, his hospitality, his sophistication, his son or his father but *not* his wife or any females in his family, since you will very rarely be allowed to meet them and this will make him feel embarrassed and un-Western. Similarly you can wax lyrical (and creative) about your company, your money, your car, your hobbies, your son or Britain but *not* about your wife, girlfriends or daughters and *not* about Israel. Arabs know that most Westerners are ambivalent about the Arab–Israeli conflict and even if you express anti-Israeli sentiments you will not be much believed. It is much better to think of it as taboo and decline to be drawn even if pressed.

In a nutshell, then, make your business trip to the Arab world worthwhile by playing the role of the sophisticated and sympathetic liberal spirit that you are and you will strike a harmonious chord with almost every one of your Arab partners in trade.

business card kaart yubàyin al-wazèefah

business trip rìHlat Àmal

businessman ràjul a'amàal

businesswoman sayìdat a'amàal

busy (*person, streets, telephone line*) mashghòol

but walàkin
   not in London but over here moo fee lòndon, walàkin hùna

butter zìbdah زبدة

button ziràar [(*pl*) azràar]

buy ishtàraa [yashtàree]
   I'll buy it! sa-ashtarèeha!

by: by train bil-qiTàar
   by plane biT-Tayàarah
   we'll have to know by . . . làazim nà'arif bi-Hulòol
. . .
   it's made by X sana'àt-ha X
Note this means literally 'X manufactured it' there being no word for 'by' in this sense (*see* PASSIVE).

C

café màqhaa

CAFÉS

The café is the hub of the social life of almost all Arab communities – together with the mosque. In the big cities pavement cafés in the European style are common, but out in the provinces the café is more like a club-house, often being built around a private courtyard. The main drinks are coffee and tea. In the café the main activity is the seemingly endless playing of backgammon, draughts and chess, the players often sitting puffing away at hubble-bubble water-pipes or **nargèelah**. Anywhere but in the largest cities, cafés are exclusively male preserves and a woman, even with a man, is likely to be constantly stared at and even reprimanded for venturing out to enjoy herself so publicly.

In the large cosmopolitan cities, such as Cairo, Alexandria and Amman, European women and children are welcomed but even so only with a man. It is fair to say that cafés – and indeed anywhere public in the Arab world – is not a place for a single woman. European women without a man really are best advised to travel around with another woman rather than on their own.

Cafés are open from around 8 in the morning to 10 at night. They do not usually serve food other than dishes of peanuts and crisps. For food you will need a stand-up pavement snack-bar or a restaurant. Although the café will not sell food itself the management will often have an arrangement with outside vendors to come in and hawk their sandwiches, gooey cakes and bags of nuts around the tables. The vendor will later pay the management a commission for the privilege.

When you leave the café, put a 10 per cent tip under your saucer for the waiter. The waiters often receive a very small wage from the café and depend on the tips for their livelihood!

When you enter a café you will usually be greeted by the manager or a waiter saying:

màrHaban!
welcome!

You might then start to say the following:

can we sit here/there?
mùmkin nàjlis hùna/hunàak?

I want a cup of coffee, please
urèed finjàan qàhwah lou samàHt

we want a cup of tea, please
nurèed finjàan shaay lou samàHt

tea with sugar
shaay maDbòot

coffee without sugar
qàhwah bidòon sùkar

we want to play chess
nurèed nàl'ab shaTràanj

we'd like to pay, please
nurèed nàdfa' lou samàHt

keep the change!
khàlee al-bàaqee!

Cairo al-qaahìrah

cake kayk

calculator àalah Hàasibah

calendar taqwèem

CALENDAR

In business affairs Arab countries use our Western solar calendar calculated in years A D. For religious, legal and state affairs, however, an Arabic lunar calendar is used in addition. This is calculated in years A H (anno hegirae) – from the year of the emigration of the prophet Muhammad to Medina from Mecca in 622 A D. The Muslim lunar calendar is some eleven days shorter than our Western calendar, so the years pass more quickly. 1989/90 A D corresponds to 1410 A H.

The Arabs call the Christian A H calendar **at-taqwèem al-meelàadee** and their own Muslim calendar **at-taqwèem al-hìjree**. If you know the A H lunar year you can find the equivalent A D year by using this formula: $AD = (AH \times .970225) + 621.54$. If you know the A D solar year you can discover the A H lunar equivalent by this formula: $AH = (AD - 621.54) \div .970025$.

call: what's it called? shoo ismàhaa?
    can I make a call to London? mùmkin àTlub lòndon?
    I'll call back later (*on phone*) sa'àTlub ba'adàyn

CALLIGRAPHY *see* ARABIC

camel jàmal

camera kaameèraa

can: can I ...? mùmkin ...?
    I can't ... maa àqdar ...
    can you ...? tàqdar ...?
    you can't ... maa tàqdar ...
    can he ...? yàqdar ...?
    he can't ... maa yàqdar ...
    can she ...? tàqdar?
    she can't ... maa tàqdar
    can we ...? nàqdar ...?
    we can't ... maa nàqdar ...
    can they ...? yàqdaroo ...?
    they can't ... maa yàqdaroo ...

Canada kànada   كندا

cancel àbTal [yùbTil]
    can I cancel it? mùmkin ubTìlhu?

capital (*money*) ra'ismàal

capital city Aasìmah

car sayàarah
    by car bis-sayàarah

car hire isti'jàar as-sayàarah   إيجار سيارة

car park mòuqif as-sayàarah

card (*business*) kart

care of Tàraf

carpet sijàadah

CARPETS
'Carpet' to an Arab means a large or small rug – not wall-to-wall fitted carpet! Since most houses have stone, tile or even dust floors, carpets are used to make the floor more interesting and, in the winter, to create warmth underfoot. Contrary to popular Western belief the carpets are almost never hung on the walls like tapestry, which would seem to an Arab

to be a waste of a good carpet which could otherwise be walked on.

You will also come across prayer-mats or **misàllah**. A **misàllah** is a small rectangular piece of carpet which Muslims kneel on when they pray, facing Mecca. They are often very ornate and intricately designed. The prayer-mat becomes a very personal possession to a devout Muslim and one **misàllah** may remain with him for life.

OR sajjaada شَبَّادة

case (*suitcase*) shànTah [(*pl*) shùnaT]

cash (*money*) fulòos
   can you cash this cheque for me? mùmkin taSrùf lee hàatha ash-shèek?

cassette kaasèet

cassette recorder jihàaz tasjèel

catch (*train, bus etc.*) làнiq [yàlнak]
   I'll catch the next train sa'àlнaq al-qiTàar ath-thàanee
   where do I catch a bus for . . .? min wayn àlнaq al-bàas li . . .?

centre màrkaz
   (*of city*) wàsaT al-madèenah

chair kùrsee [(*pl*) karàasee]

chairman (*of company*) ra'èes màjlis al-idàarah

CHAIRS

In the big cities you will find chairs everywhere – just as in the West. However, when you get away to the more remote villages – or stay with Bedouins in the desert – you will find that people tend to sit on cushions on the floor to relax and eat rather than sitting on chairs.

change: can I change some money? mùmkin uнàwil bà'aD al-Aùmlah?
   could you give me some small change for this? mùmkin ta'aтèenee khùrdah li hàaza?
   do I have to change trains? hal làazim ughàyir al-qiTàar?
   I'd like to change my flight urèed ughàyir mee'àad as-sàfar
   (*noun*) **we've made some changes to the design** sawàyna bà'aD at-ta'adeelàat fee at-taSmèem

cheap rakhèes
  it's cheap hàaza rakhèes

check: I'll check it sa'afHàs-ha
  could you please check that? mùmkin tafHàs-ha lou
  samàHt?

cheerio mà'as-salàamah (*literally: with peace*)

  A shorter form is: **salàam**.

cheers (*toast*) fee siHàtak

CHEERS
fee siHàtak is the toast used when drinking alcohol
and is said when the drinks have been served and
everyone is about to pick up their cup or glass. It
means literally 'to your health' and when the
proposer of the toast has said it you lift your cup or
glass and say it yourself.

cheese jìbnah جبنة

chemist's Saydalèeyah صيدلى

cheque sheek
  can I pay by cheque? mùmkin àdfa' bi-shèek?

cheque book dàftar sheekàat

cheque card biTàaqat ash-shèek

CHEQUES
In the Arab world everyone tends to use cash.
Except in places catering mainly for foreigners you
cannot use a cheque to pay for a meal, buy petrol or
fix your car. Apart from travellers cheques, which
are encashable at big banks, the only cheques you
are likely to encounter are those transferring money
between businesses. At the personal level all Arab
countries are still basically cash economies.

chest (*of body*) sadr

chicken dajàaj

children aTfàal

CHILDREN
Children are kept close to the family when they are
young and, even after graduating from college or
university, often stay under the family roof for years
– at least until they get married and set up home on
their own. Unless the family is prosperous, newly

wed couples may set up home in a part of their parents' house and become part of an extended family. In general, parents are very indulgent of their children, as in many Mediterranean countries, and old people are never left alone in their declining years as they are in many Western societies. Elderly parents become the reponsibility of their sons, especially of the eldest son.

chips baτàaτis maqlèeyah

chocolate shokoolàatah

Christian name ism

CHRISTIAN NAMES

When you are in the Arab world it is best not to talk about Christian names and surnames but 'first names' and 'family names'. Since the very great majority of Arabs are not Christian, offence and certainly confusion may be caused by referring to Christian names. First and family name is a convenient device for getting somebody's name right since everybody in the Arab world and the West has at least one of each (*see* ADDRESSING PEOPLE).

Christmas Aèed al-meelàad

CHRISTMAS

Christmas is not celebrated by Muslims at all. In Christian communities, however, such as the Egyptian Copts and the Lebanese Maronites, Christmas is celebrated as a major festival just as it is in the West.

church kinèesah

CHURCHES

In Lebanon and Egypt, where there are large native Christian communities, churches are found in most towns and all cities. In Egypt these will be Coptic and in Lebanon Maronite. In addition there are small communities of Armenian, Greek and Russian Orthodox Christians in many countries and these groups have their own churches. In large cities, where there are a number of resident foreigners, there are Anglican and Catholic churches used mainly by those foreign residents and any other visiting foreigners.

cigar seegàar

cigarette sigàarah

cine-camera àalat taswèer seenimaa'èeyah

cinema as-sèenimaa

city madèenah [(*pl*) mùdun]

city centre wàsat al-madèenah

clean (*adjective*) nazèef

clock sà'ah kabèerah

closed maqfòol

clothes malàabis

CLOTHING

It is difficult to generalize about clothing anywhere, but let us consider firstly the Arabian Peninsula and the Gulf and secondly Egypt and the other Mediterranean countries.

In the Peninsula, the usual dress for men is a white garment called a **dishdàasha** and a large white cloth placed over the head called a **ghùTrah**. This is secured by a thick black rope called an **Aqàal**. Underneath the **dishdàasha** a sort of waist-toga called a **wizàar** is worn. These white clothes are perfect for reflecting the great heat usually prevailing in those parts. Outside the Peninsula men wear normal Western clothes, often with a head-cloth to keep off the sun.

Women in the Peninsula will wear a normal frock called a **fustàan** and over this a heavy black garment called an **ubàayah**. They cover their faces, when they leave the house to go shopping, with a black veil called a **Hijàab**. This is the only time they go out of the house unless they are going to the doctor or dentist or making a social visit.

In Egypt, Lebanon, and Syria for many years now women have worn Western-style dresses and frocks cut fairly modestly. However, now that Islamic fervour is coming back into favour, in all these countries, and indeed in the whole region of the Near and Middle East, the black **ubàayah** and veil worn in the Gulf are also making a strong comeback and in most cases anyway it is the women's way of asserting their Islamic identity and their rejection of some Western moral values.

Western male visitors to the Peninsula should wear long trousers and not shorts in the street – which makes sense anyway for most of the year when the sun is scorchingly hot. A woman visiting the Peninsula should wear a midi- or full-length skirt – not trousers – on her occasional forays out of the house with her husband.

Outside the Peninsula, in Egypt, Syria, Iraq and the other Mediterranean Arab states, women should wear 'modest' and 'decorous' clothes, which means at least half-length sleeves and skirts below the knee. A head-scarf is often good protection against the sun and this is the way Arab women protect themselves from the heat, dust and sun.

Bikinis or anything skimpy or remotely see-through are absolutely out for women – or men come to that – except in the privacy of their (large) hotel.
See also WEATHER

coat balТòo

code (*dialling*) ràqm fatн al-khàт

coffee qàhwah   قهوة
  white coffee qàhwah bil-нalèeb

COFFEE

Black coffee is **qàhwah** and is the norm in the Arab world. It is usually made very strong and sweet and flavoured with cardamom. It is served in small finger-cups – which are small china bowls with no handle held between two fingers of the (right) hand – with a glass of iced water. If you want white coffee you must ask for coffee with milk **qàhwah bil-нalèeb** and expect everyone in the café to look at you.

Coffee and tea are the main beverages drunk socially – not alcohol as in the West. If you visit someone's house, even on a very short call, you will be offered a choice of tea or coffee. By convention you always accept one or the other even if it is the last thing you want. You could always plead severe indigestion, but then you will get an Alka Seltzer and a glass of warm milk!
See also INSTANT COFFEE

coin Aùmlah
See MONEY

cold (*adjective*) bàarid
   it's cold al-jòu bàarid
   I've got a cold Àndee zukàam

colour loun

colour film film mulòuwan

comb (*noun*) mishT

come jaa
   he's coming tomorrow sayàjee bùkrah
   I come from . . . àna min . . .
   when are you coming to England? ìmta satàjee li-ingiltìra?

committed: we are committed to the project ìHna multazimèen bil-mashròoA

company (*business*) shìrkah

COMPARISON OF ADJECTIVES

The comparative and superlative of adjectives – big, bigger, biggest, small, smaller, smallest – are formed by a complicated internal change. To form the comparative of most adjectives an **a-** is added at the beginning and the vowels in the word are changed to **a**. For example:

big	kabèer	**bigger**	àkbar
small	saghèer	**smaller**	àsghar
poor	faqèer	**poorer**	àfqar
rich	ghanèe	**richer**	àghna

To form the superlative an **al-** is added to the comparative. For example:

the biggest	al-àkbar
the smallest	al-àsghar
the poorest	al-àfqar
the richest	al-àghna
the cheapest	al-àrkhas
the most expensive	al-àghla

Both these forms are often used just to mean 'very' big/small/poor/rich etc.

The famous Muslim call to prayer which you can hear from the minaret of a mosque at prayer-time starts with the words:

allàhu àkbar

which means:

Allah is very great/the greatest.

To say 'X is bigger than Y' or 'A is smaller than B' you use the above forms followed by **min** as the comparative particle 'than':

X is bigger than Y
X àkbar min Y

A is smaller than B
A àsghar min B

he is taller than me
hùwa àTwal mìnee

that house is more expensive than this one
zàalik al-bàyt àghla min hàaza

competitive (*prices*) munàafis

complaint shàkwah

computer kompeeyòotir

conditions (*of contract*) shuròoT

conference (*full-scale conference such as the UN etc.*) mu'atàmar
(*company meeting*) ijtimàa'

conference room (*in hotel etc.*) ghùrfat al-ijtimaa'àt

consignment (*of goods*) shùHnah

constipation imsàak

consul qùnsul
the British consul al-qùnsul al-breeTàanee

contact: I'll get in contact with him àna sa'atàsil bih
where can I contact you? wayn àqdar atàsil bik?

contact lenses Adasàat laasìqah

container (*for shipping*) wi'àa'

contract (*noun*) Aqd

cool (*weather*) bàarid

corkscrew barèemah

corner rukn
in the corner feer-rùkn
at the corner And ar-rùkn

correct (*adjective*) saHèeH
that's correct hàaza saHèeH

cost (*noun*) taklìfah
what does it cost? àyesh yatakàlaf?

let's look at the costs khàlna nashòof at-taklìfah
the cost of . . . taklìfat al-. . .

cotton wool qùтun тìbee

could: could I . . .? mùmkin a . . .?
    could you . . .? mùmkin ta . . .?
    could I see? mùmkin ashòof?

country (*nation*) bàlad [(*pl*) buldàan]

couple: a couple of . . . zouj min . . .

course: of course! tàb'an!

crazy hàaza
    that's crazy hàadha jèenan

cream (*for face*, *food*, *coffee*) kreem

credit card biтàaqat i'timàan
    I've lost my credit cards faqàdtu biтaaqàatee al-
    i'timàan

CREDIT CARDS
    Like cheques, credit cards are not widely recognized
    away from tourist haunts. Arab countries still have
    cash economies and as long as this remains so, credit
    cards will be rarely seen.

crisis àzmah

crisps baтàaтis sheeps

crowd zàнmah

crowded muzdàнim

cultural exchange at-tabaadùl ath-thaqàafee

cup finajàan [(*pl*) fanaaji]
    a cup of tea finajàan shaay

CUPS
    Tea and coffee are usually drunk out of small
    finger-cups (or glasses). These cups are small, white
    china cups with no handles and are held between
    the thumb and forefinger of the (right) hand.
    Sometimes they stand in small holders of beaten
    copper or brass.

cushion wisàadah

CUSHIONS

Cushions are used on furniture just as they are in the West. In the Arabian Peninsula, however, most houses have a room which is used especially for guests and which is called a **màjlis**. This is usually a large room within a short distance of the main door. It will have several layers of carpets and rows of cushions along the sides of the room. There are no chairs. People simply prop themselves up on the cushions.

When you are sitting around socially on cushions or just on a mat the best position to be in is cross-legged – you probably last tried it at primary school, in which case you will probably need a lot of practice! Arabs are so used to it it comes naturally to them and they will not appreciate your difficulty. Women who always wear skirts socially should never think of attempting it in Arab company.

A good compromise for everybody is to fold your legs tightly to one side, even under the cushion, making it look as if you have been doing it since you were a toddler. Whatever you do keep your feet behind you and away from any food or drink that may be in front of you. Squatting is something that only beggars do and is very rude.

custom Aadà
Arab customs Aadàat Arabèeyah

CUSTOM

Custom or **urf** is as important today in many Arab countries, especially in the Arabian Peninsula, as it was in Europe during the Middle Ages. If something is done by 'custom' it has the ultimate sanction of tradition, which gives it such great authority that innovative rulers and governments in that region have to tread very warily. Arab customs regarding women and their status and alcohol consumption, for example, are inextricably bound up in the traditions of Islam and are defended principally by the Muslim elders. Arabs who travel to the West are frequently astonished that reforming man-made laws, Acts of Parliament for example, are accepted by society merely because they are laws. Muslim societies are based on the different premise that Allah is the only law-giver and only He need really be obeyed.

customer (*of company*) zabòon [(*pl*) zabàa'in]
   you're a very important customer ànta zabòon
   muhìm jìdan

Customs jùmrok   جمرك

D

dam sad

danger khàTar خطر

dark (*no light*) mò'tem
(*colour*) dàaken

date ta'arèekh
See CALENDAR, NUMBERS

Some useful phrases are:

> **what is the date today?**
> aysh at-ta'arèekh al-yòum?

> **today is the first of January**
> al-yòum al-àwal min yanàayeer

> **today is the seventh of April**
> al-yòum as-sàabiʌ min ibrèel

daughter ìbnah

day youm

DAYS

The Arabic week starts on Friday at sunset. The days
of the week are:

Saturday	youm as-sàbt
	(*literally: the Sabbath day*)
Sunday	youm al-àHad
	(*day one*)
Monday	youm al-ithnàyn
	(*day two*)
Tuesday	youm ath-thulathàa
	(*day three*)
Wednesday	youm al-arba'àa
	(*day four*)
Thursday	youm al-khamèes
	(*day five*)
Friday	youm al-jùm'ah
	(*day of assembly (in the mosque)*)

Some useful phrases are:

> **what day is it today?**
> ay al-ayàam al-yòum?

> **today is Wednesday**
> al-yòum youm al-arba'àa

today is Sunday
al-yòum youm al-àHad

on Monday
youm al-ithnàyn

since Friday
mùnzu youm al-jùm'ah

dead màyit

deal (*in business*) Sàfqah
it's a deal! itafaqna!

December deesìmbir

declare: nothing to declare maa fee shay yastàHiq aD-DDarèebah

delay (*of plane etc.*) ta'akhèer
(*postponement*) ta'ajèel
he's been delayed hùwa ta'àkhar

delicious lazèez

If you have just enjoyed a delicious meal you can say:

akl mumtàaz! Good food!

dentist Tabèeb asnàan

dentures Tàqim asnàan

desert saHàraa'

diarrhoea is-hàal

diary mufakìrah

dictionary qaamòos

difference ikhtilàaf
the main difference al-ikhtilàaf ar-ra'èesee
it doesn't make any difference kùluh wàaHid

different mukhtàlif

difficult sà'ab

difficulty suAòobah

DIMINUTIVES

These are very rare in Arabic and are usually only used as terms of endearment. Here are some examples:

dog	kalb
doggy	kulàyb
cat	qaT
kitty	quTàyta

my son	ìbni
my little boy	bunàya

dinner al-Ashàa

DINNER
Dinner is eaten late by Western standards, from 8 to 11 p.m. It is not as substantial as lunch, which is also eaten late, and the food will tend to be spicy and exotic (contrasting with the rather more filling lunches, with pasta, rice and bread). Offices and shops often re-open between 5 and 7.30 p.m. and dinner will be eaten after that. Whereas lunch is primarily a family affair, dinner is the occasion for eating out or with friends.

direct (*flight etc.*) mubàashir

director mudèer [(*pl*) mudaràa]

dirty qàzir

disadvantage Ayb [(*pl*) Ayòob]

discount (*noun*) takhfèeD

discussion niqàash

dish (*plate*) Tàbaq
(*meal*) wàjbah

diskette usToowàanah màrinah mumàghnaTah
on diskette àla usToowàanah (màrinah mumàgh-naTah)

distance masàafah
what's the distance from . . . to . . .? àyesh al-masàafah bayn . . . li . . .?

DISTANCE
Distance in the Arab world is always measured in metres and kilometres. Miles are known as a unit of distance but are not used. Arabs do not have a very precise sense of distance and, if asked how far two places are apart, tend to reply that it is the same as between Alexandria and Cairo, or between this village and the one over the hill.

distribution (*of goods*) touwzèeA

divorced Tàlaq

do Àmal [yà'amal]
can you do that? hal tàqdar tà'amal hàaza?

doctor Tabèeb; dùktoor دكتور

DOCTORS

Tabèeb is a professional medical man and **dùktoor** is his title or the title of an academic who has obtained a doctorate – a rare and very prestigious thing in the Arab world. As in all parts of the developing world, and even in the developed world, there are the extremes of medical care – from the most modern medical facilities to bare-foot doctors in the remote villages. Medical attention in most Arabic countries is a private affair and expensive, although some countries, such as the United Arab Emirates and Saudi Arabia, do have free hospital and health care.

document wathèeqah [(*pl*) wathàa'iq]

door baab [(*pl*) abwàab]

double: double gin jin doobl
double room ghùrfah bi-sareeràyn

down àsfal
the price has come down as-sìAr inkhàfaD

down payment Arbòon

draft (*of agreement*) musòuwadah

dress (*noun: woman's*) fustàan [(*pl*) fasaatèen]
See CLOTHING

drink (*noun*) mashròob
would you like a drink? tuHìb tàshrab shay?
thanks but I don't drink shùkran, walàkin àna maa àshrab

DRINK

If Arabs do like to drink, they do so only with close friends or at home. They very rarely drink in public. Even if someone drinks like a fish he tends to say no to drink offered by a stranger. *See also* ALCOHOL.

driving licence rùkhsat qeeyàadah

drunk (*adjective*) sakràan

DRUNKENNESS

It is very rare to see Arabs in the Arab world drunk, as their society is very disapproving of drunkenness. And, as the Koran forbids it, few people drink at all. In the Peninsula states, drunkenness is punishable by public whipping, foreigners often included. In whichever area they are travelling, Westerners are best advised to give their livers a rest and enjoy the huge range of mineral drinks and fruit juices that are available everywhere.

dry jaaf

dry-cleaner's maghsàlah

dune kathèeb [(*pl*) kuthbàan]

during athnàa

E

each kul
  how much are they each? (*masc.*) bikàm kul wàaHid?
  (*fem.*) bikàm kul waaHìdah?
  each of them kul wàaHid/kul waaHìdah mìnhum

ear ùzun

early (*arrive*) bàdree
  early in the morning bàdree fees-sabàaH

east ash-shàrq
  in the East feesh-shàrq

Easter Aèed al-fùs-H

EASTER
Easter is not celebrated by Muslims at all. In
Christian communities, however, such as the Egyptian Copts and the Lebanese Maronites, Easter is
celebrated as a major festival just as it is in the West.

easy sahl

eat àkal [yà'kul]
  something to eat shay lil-'àkl

EATING HABITS
Eating habits in the Arab world vary according to
country. In Egypt and Lebanon, countries where
Western influence has been great in the past, food is
presented on individual plates for each person.
Knives and forks are used, and both hands are used
to wield them. A Western visitor would have no
difficulty feeling at ease in these countries.
   On the other hand in the Peninsula states – such
as Saudi Arabia, the Yemens, Qatar, Kuwait, Bahrain, Oman and the United Arab Emirates – dining
takes quite a different form. Here food arrives served
directly on large trays and the male members of the
family and their guests sit round the tray and help
themselves – only using their right hand, and
without using any cutlery except perhaps a spoon for
unmanageable items. The left hand is considered
unclean and must never be used for helping yourself
with. In fact it is best to do what most Arabs in those
countries do and keep your left hand behind your

back! This only applies to meals taken in private homes. In all restaurants and hotels throughout the Arab world food is served Western-style on individual plates, although the plates may well be with you on a mat on the floor. For goodness sake don't take any notice of the fallacious myth that it is right and proper to belch and/or pass wind after a meal to signify appreciation of the food.

See also BREAKFAST, DINNER, FOOD, LUNCH, RESTAURANTS

economy iqtisàad
  the Arab economy al-iqtisàad al-Àrabee

Egypt misr

Egyptian (*adjective*, *noun*) mìsree

either ay
  either one ay wàaHid
  either ... or ... ìma ... ou ...

electric kahrabàa'ee

electronics iliktroneeyàat

else: something else shay àakhar
  somewhere else makàan àakhar

embarrassing mùkhjil

EMBARRASSMENT

It is fair to say that all the things, big and small, which Westerners find embarrassing will also seem embarrassing to Arabs. This covers the whole range of embarrassing moments arising from being caught out saying one thing and doing another to lambasting the character and motives of people who later turn out to be among the people you have just been addressing.

Two things are most likely to cause embarrassment: sex and women. Most Western businessmen and travellers can take a fair amount of frank discussion on these subjects at an appropriate moment without cringing unduly, but even an Arab man-of-the-world will turn absolutely puce at the mere hint of extra-marital relations and be plunged into embarrassed confusion at even the most inadvertent glimpse of any substantial amount of female flesh. Similarly what may be related as a harmless if slightly risqué joke by a Westerner will probably seem unbelievably ribald to an Arab hearer and quite unworthy of anybody he likes to think of as an equal. Another subject to be avoided is negative aspersions cast on the sanity or other attributes of your mother-in-law, grandmother or assorted aunts. Arabs are deeply respectful of senior members of their family (and other families) and your light-hearted banter will make your Arab hearer feel that there is a badly concealed harsh streak to your human relations.

If an Arab is embarrassed by something you have said or done you will surely know this by the sudden onset of undisguised blushing and silence. Silence is the danger sign in all your dealings with Arabs and may arise from embarrassment, anger or plain bewilderment. Not for Arabs the bravura cover-up of loquacious Western businessmen – just silence.

embassy sifàarah
   the British embassy as-sifàarah al-briTaanèeyah

empty (*adjective*) fàaDee

end (*noun: of period of time, of road*) nihàayah

engineer muhàndis

England ingiltìra   انجلترا

English (*adjective*) inglèezee
   (*language*) al-lùghah al-ingleezèeyah
   I'm English (*man*) àna inglèezee
   (*woman*) àna ingleezèeyah
   do you speak English? hal tatakàlam inglèezee?

ENGLISH

English is now the second language of the great majority of Arab countries and is usually also the second language of government notices and publications. It is very widely taught in private and state schools and it is fair to say that most educated Arabs who comprise the commercial and political élites in each country speak and understand a reasonable amount of English, usually enough to discuss non-technical business deals. The predominance of English as a second language has become complete only since the Second World War and the ascendancy of the United States as the centre of the business world. Before the war French was the second language of those Arab countries within its political orbit – such

as Syria and Algeria – and even today older people
there may speak only Arabic and French.

Nowadays there is a growing number of private
schools in many Arab cities which carry out all
tuition in English. And in larger hotels and restaurants there will always be someone who speaks some
basic English.

enough kàafee
not enough moo kàafee
that's enough, thank you hàaza kàafee shùkran

entrance dukhòol   دخول

envelope zarf

essential Daròoree
that's essential hàaza Daròoree
no, that's not essential la, hàaza moo Daròoree

estimate (*noun*) taqdèer
it's only an estimate hàaza taqdèer fàqaT

Europe ooròoba
in Europe fee ooròoba

evening masàa
this evening hàaza al-masàa
good evening masàa al-khàyr

every kul

everyone al-jamèeA
hello everyone! as-salàam Alàykum

This all-purpose greeting **as-salàam Alàykum** means
literally 'peace be upon you'. This phrase is always
appropriate when meeting people be it for a meal, a
wedding, a funeral or a ministerial conference.

everything kul shay
well, I think that's everything (*said at end of meeting
etc.*) shùkran Àla istimà' akum

excellent mumtàaz
excellent! azèem!/mumtàaz!

azèem! is used to mean 'great!', 'wonderful!' in
general; **mumtàaz** means something particular, some
particular job has been done very well.

exchange rate sìAr at-taHwèel
what is the exchange rate for the pound? aysh sìAr
at-taHwèel lil-jinèeyah?

excuse me (*to get attention*) min fàDlak
(*apology*) àasif
excuse me, could you tell me where . . .? lou samàHt,
mùmkin taqòol lee wayn . . .?

exhausted: I'm exhausted àna ta'abàan

exhibition (*trade fair etc.*) mà'araD

exit khuròoj خروج

expenses maSàareef
it's on expenses hìya Àlal-masàareef

expensive ghàalee

expiry date (*of visa etc.*) ta'arèekh al-intihàa

explain shàraH [yìshraH]
could you explain that to me? mùmkin tishràH lee
hàaza?

export (*verb*) sàdar [yusàdir]
we export . . . ìHna nusàdir . . .
our export campaign Hamlàtna lit-tasdèer

export director mudèer at-tasdèer

express: by express mail bil-barèed al-mustà'ajil

express train geTàar sarèe

expression (*on face*) ta'abèer

extension: extension 334 taHwèelah ràqam 334
(*of contract*) tamdèed

extra iDàafee
there are no extra charges maa fee rusòom
iDaafèeyah
is that extra? hal hàaza iDàafee?

eye Ayn

eye contact al-itisàal bil-Aynàyn

EYE CONTACT
Eye contact is very important when meeting Arab
men: look them straight in the eye as much as you
can. It is considered the friendly and honest thing to
do and will be reciprocated. Like Italians and
Greeks, Arabs 'talk with their eyes' and will be at
ease if you do so too. If you spend your time looking
at the floor or your finger-nails they will feel you
have something to hide. Direct eye-to-eye contact
does not ever have the insolent overtones it can have
in the West. When meeting Arab women, however,

the opposite is true. Women do not figure at all prominently in Arab professional society but if you are introduced to a woman do not look her in the eye. She will have been brought up to avert her gaze from a man, especially a foreigner-stranger, so do not embarrass her or the men around her by trying to look into her face.

F

face wajh

factory màsna'

fair (*commercial*) mà'araD

fall (*verb*) (*person*) sàqaT [yàsquT]
   sales are falling mabi'àatna inkhafàDat

family Aahìlah
   my family Aahìlatee

FAMILY

Children in the Arab world keep up much stronger
ties with their families than is common in the West.
Sons and daughters continue to live in the family
home until they get married and if they have
difficulty finding a home for themselves one of the
two parent families will almost certainly welcome
them into their home – sometimes for ever. Whereas
in the West the aim of most young people is to set up
on their own in their twenties this urge is simply not
present in Arab young people. The nearer they can
stay to the bosom of their family the luckier they
consider themselves. It has to be said that, in the
frequent absence of any form of state-sponsored
social security arrangements, the family represents a
safe haven and a natural springboard for social
achievement. Many prospective or actual parents
build their own house in the form of two or three
flatlets so their children will have somewhere to live
when they grow up and marry.

far ba'èed
   how far is it to . . .? aysh al-masàafah ìla . . .?
   is it far? hal hìya ba'èedah?

Far East ash-shàrq al-àqsaa

fast sarèeA
   too fast sarèeA jìdan
   (*in a dangerous way*) bi-Tarèeqah khaTèerah

father ab

faulty (*equipment*) bìha khàlal

fax (*noun*) faaks

February fibràayeer

feel shà'ar [tàshAor]
    how are you feeling? kayf tàshAor?
    I'm feeling better àshAor bi-taHassùn
    I feel like a . . . (*drink etc.*) àshAor bi-Hàaja ìla . . .

FEMININE FORMS

In general the feminine ending of a word is **-ah**. A
masculine noun can be made feminine simply by
adding the feminine ending **-ah** to it as a suffix. For
example:

mudèer	manager
mudèerah	manageress
mu'àawin	assistant
mu'aawìnah	assistant
muDèef	(airline) steward
muDèefah	(airline) stewardess

Many common words are feminine in their own
right. Of course they then only have a feminine
form. For example:

madèenah	city
maHkàmah	court (of law)
jazèerah	island

There are some words which are feminine but
which do not have the feminine **-ah** ending. Among
these are words which are:

logically feminine:

um	mother
bint	girl

names of most cities and countries:

misr	Egypt (or Cairo)
soorèeya	Syria
barèes	Paris

most parts of the body:

yad	hand
Ayn	eye
rijl	leg

All these words are grammatically feminine and if
they are associated with adjectives or verbs these
must agree with them.
See AGREEMENT, NOUNS

ferry mu'adìyah

few shuwàyah
  just a few bas shuwàyah
  a few days bÌDAt ayàam

figure (*number*) ràqam
  can we see the figures? mùmkin nashòof al-arqàam?
  See also NUMBERS

filling (*in tooth*) Hàshwoo

film (*for camera, at cinema*) film

final nihàa'ee
  that's our final offer hàaza hùwa ARàDna an-nihàa'ee

finance director mudèer màalee

find wàjad [yàjid]

fine Tàyib
  that's fine hàaza Tàyib

finger ùsbuA

finish intàha [yantàhi]
  I haven't finished (*meal etc.*) maa intahàytu

fire (*for heating*) naar
  (*destructive*) Harèeq

first (*adjective*) àwal
  See DATES

first class (*travel etc.*) dàrajah òolah

first name ism

FIRST NAMES
Your first name is the name you will be known by in the Arab world. Arabs use surnames only to differentiate between people having the same first name. Do not be afraid of using first names to people you have just met. This will be considered perfectly normal and not over-friendly as it might be in the West.

fish (*noun*) sàmak سمك

flat (*apartment*) shàqah

flight rìHlat aT-Tayaràan
  my flight is at . . . Tayaaràtee as-sàa'ah . . .

flight number ràqam ar-rìHlah

floor arDèeyah
  on the third/fourth floor feeT-Tàabiq ath-thàalith/ar-ràabiA

FLOORS
Most houses in the Arab world have stone or tiled floors to keep the rooms fairly cool in summer.

These are often covered with carpets (*see* CARPETS) or rugs in cool weather or when guests arrive. While some living-rooms have sofas ranged around the walls to sit on, in some Gulf countries cushions are just piled up on the floor Bedouin-style and guests prop themselves up against them while actually sitting on the floor itself.

flower zàhr [(*pl*) zùhur]
    a bunch of flowers bàaqat zùhur

flu inflooèenzaa

fly (*verb*) Taar [yaTèer]

food Ta'àam طعام

FOOD
All large hotels and restaurants serve a wide range of (usually) excellent European and American food. But if you are an adventurous eater you will find in Arab cooking a whole new range of tastes and preparations, a large part of which is an amalgam of the cuisine of other Mediterranean countries such as Spain, Italy, Greece and Turkey. These culinary traditions have not merely been copied but have been improved upon and the result is a distinctive 'Arab' cuisine. The only food you will never see in the Arab world is pork, which is forbidden by the Koran.

Obviously no list of dishes can be completely comprehensive but here is some of the more distinctively Arab fare you may encounter on your menu. You will find that the secret to Arab cooking is an extensive use of yoghurt, saffron and peppers – often as a background to other more obvious ingredients.

You may well want to start your meal with a starter or **muqabilàat**.

STARTERS

Hùmus	a thick spicy paste made from ground chick-peas and oil – usually served with salad and pitta bread
batàarikh	a very pungent red caviar
tabòolah	a mixed salad made from mint, cracked

	wheat, watercress and parsley
bàba ghanòoj	smoked aubergine with **тaнèenah**
тaнèenah	a thick sesame dip – usually served with pitta bread and salad

Whatever you are eating you will probably want some bread (*see* BREAD). Bread in the Arab world, as in Greece and Turkey, is unleavened. This makes a small amount very substantial since there is no air in it to raise it. The usual name for this bread is now well-known in the West – pitta or **bèetah** as Arabs pronounce it.

If you have any room left after the starter you may want a main course, perhaps sea-food or fish, which is always caught locally. If you are far from the sea or rivers it will be unavailable – frozen fish is unheard of.

FISH

istaakòoza	lobster
kaaboorèeya	crab
jàmbaree	shrimp
sàmak màshwee	grilled fish
sàmak màqlee	fried fish
sàmak feel-fòrn	baked fish
sayaadèeyah	sort of risotto made with whatever fish is to hand

Or perhaps meat (don't bother looking for pork: it is forbidden by the Koran – lamb is the most popular).

MEAT

Dàanee	lamb
bitìloo	veal
bàqaree	beef

Some specialities include:

kharòof màHshee	stuffed lamb
kòoskus	couscous, a thick lamb stew with a semolina base
maqlòobah	meat and aubergine stew with rice
mùzat	veal stew
kùftah	meat-balls

Or there is poultry:

firàakh	chicken
buT	duck
Hamàam	pigeon
wiz	goose
Tàajin tufàaya	boiled chicken with saffron
firàakh bil-khàlTah	roast chicken with rice and nuts
biràam Hamàam	pigeon baked in milk

VEGETABLES

As in most Mediterranean countries – and elsewhere nowadays – vegetables are often served as a main course:

banadòorah	tomato
baTàaTis	potatoes
baazinjàan	aubergines
TumàaTim	tomatoes
jàzar	carrots
fool	broad beans
bàsal	onions
loòbiya	runner beans
khiyàar	cucumbers

DESSERTS

Arab desserts are very sweet even by Western standards and syrup is a main ingredient of most of them. Some of the common ones you may come across are:

kunàafah	shredded wheat with syrup
basbòosah	semolina baked in butter and syrup
baqlàawah	pastry layered with nuts and soaked in syrup
balòozah	thick mousse with nuts
bàlaH ash-shàam	dates of Damascus – not real dates but pas-

try pieces deep-fried in
oil and syrup

If you still have more room, finish off with fruit,
which is widely available, locally grown and always
cheap.

FRUIT

mìshmish	apricots
mooz	bananas
kirìz	cherries
tamr	dates
khookh	peaches
shammam	melon
teen	figs
burtuqàal	oranges
barqòoq	plums
ànab	grapes
romàan	pomegranate
manjah	mango

Any fresh fruit or vegetables bought in a market
should always, of course, be thoroughly cleaned.

Coffee or tea will be served after the meal but tea
is much more common, unlike in the West where
coffee is the rule after food. Do not light up a
cigarette or settle down with a **nargèelah** (water-
pipe) straight after the meal: wait and see how your
host plays it. You are more likely to be challenged to
a game of chess or draughts – Arabs are experienced
gamesmen and unless you are extremely good at
chess you will almost certainly be beaten hands
down by your Arab opponents, including those of
tender years.

foot (*on body*) qàdam

for (*with periods of time*) li-mùdah
   for three nights li-mùdah thalàath layàalee
   this is for you hàaza lak
   that's for me hàaza lee
   that's for us hàaza làna
   are you for the idea? hal ànta muwàafiq?

foreign ajnàbee

foreign exchange (*money*) at-taHwèel al-khàarijee

foreigner (*man*) ajnàbee
   (*woman*) ajnabèeyah

forget nàsa/yànsa
   I forget ànsa

I didn't forget maa nasàytu
I forgot my briefcase here nasàytu shanTàtee hùna

fork (*for eating*) shòukah

FORKS
In Mediterranean Arab countries the fork is used
with a knife and spoon to eat with just as in the West.
In the Peninsula states, such as Saudi Arabia,
Kuwait, Bahrain, Qatar, Oman and the Yemens,
however, where meals are normally served from one
dish, the spoon will be the only piece of cutlery used
for eating. And often, even when guests are present,
the spoon is dispensed with and the right hand is
used as the main 'piece of cutlery'.

formal (*dinner, occasion*) ràsmee

FORMALITY
Apart from prayers, there are no occasions when you
will be expected to act more formally than you
would normally do in the West. On the contrary,
Western formality at meals and meetings is a
common object of Arab humour.

free (*no cost*) majàanan

freight (*noun*) shaHn

Friday youm al-jùm'ah

FRIDAY
This is the traditional Muslim day of rest when all
government offices will be closed.

fridge thalàajah

friend sadèeq

FRIENDS
Apart from his wife, the only friends an Arab man is
going to have are men, friendship between the sexes
being considered the first step down the slippery
slope of uncontrolled debauchery. You will, if you
are a man, find a very strong sense of camaraderie
among Arabs and it is a high compliment indeed to
be welcomed into a group of Arab men as 'one of the
brothers'. In a virtually all-male social climate Arabs
seem to spend all their emotional energy on other
men, resulting in often intense displays of rivalry,
jealousy, vengefulness, loyalty and affection, not

necessarily in that order. A friendly Arab will often call you simply **ya akhèe!** (my brother!) instead of using your name and this demonstrates the reality of inter-Arab relationships. In an Arab's mind the world consists of Arab brothers, foreigners and foreign visitors who, if they read this book well, will become honorary brothers for the length of their stay at least! Things are clear-cut: you are either a friend or an enemy – and equally a friend or an enemy of the Arabs in general. On your trip to the Arab world it is wisest to wear your heart on your sleeve and make it clear you are the former.

from min
    from here to ... min hùna ìla ...
    this is a present from us hàazee hidàyah mìna
    from next month min ash-shàhr al-jàayee

front amàam
    in front of my hotel amàam fùnduqee

fruit fawàaкah فاكهة
    See FOOD

FRUIT

Apart from all the fruit you are used to seeing in the West, you will notice a lot of pomegranates and mangoes. You are strongly advised to eat no more than one a day of either of these if you want to get out of your hotel at all during your visit.

Although much of the Arab world is a desert the very warm climate prevailing throughout the region for most of the year means that, given adequate irrigation, two or even three crops of fruit and vegetables can be harvested each year. Therefore each plot of land produces so much that the population of, for example, Egypt is entirely kept in fruit and vegetables.

full (*hotel etc.*) maнjòoz
    no thanks, I'm full laa shùkran, àna shab'àan

Wherever you go socially in the Arab world you will be offered some form of refreshment, often syrupy and solid, even if you have just arrived from a full meal. It is the Arab custom to accept at least some of whatever you are offered and it can be offensive to say you are 'full up'. The wisest policy is to undereat until late in the evening!

fun: it's fun hàaza zarèef

funny (*strange*) gharèeb
(*comical*) mùDHik

furniture mafrooshàat

FURNITURE

Modern Western-style furniture is being used more and more in the Arab world. But you will often find, if you are visiting socially, that a special guest-room is furnished in the Western style while the other living-rooms just have carpets and cushions around them. A helpful hint for Western visitors: try to find a way of sitting on the ground which is comfortable for long periods before you set out for the Arab world. You may well have to join your Arab colleagues on the carpeted floor somewhere during your visit and eat a full meal in that position. It is best to plan for this contingency in advance.

further àb'ad
is it much further? hal hìya àb'ad bi-kathèer?

future mustàqbal
in future feel-mustàqbal

FUTURE TENSE

Using the information we have given for each verb in this book, it is easy for you to form the future tense of that verb. For example:

write kàtab [yàktub]

The second form given in square brackets is the masculine singular of the future tense minus the future prefix **sa-**, so:

sa-yàktub
he will write

From this you can work out any form of the future tense: 'I shall write' etc. using the following rules and always prefixing the verb with the characteristic future marker:

I shall write
sa-àktub   omit the **y**

you will write (*masc.*)
sa-tàktub   replace the **y** with **t**

you will write (*fem.*)
sa-taktùbee   replace **y** with **t** and add **-ee**

he will write
sa-yàktub

she will write
sa-tàktub   replace the **y** with **t** (same as
                   you will write (*masc.*))

we shall write
sa-nàktub   replace **y** with **n**

you will write (*pl*)
sa-tàktuboo   replace **y** with **t** and add -**oo**

they will write
sa-yàktuboo   add -**oo**

The personal pronoun is important with **sa-tàktub** –
unless you put **hìya** (she) or **ànta** (you) before the
verb the meaning can be confusing:

she will write the letter this morning
hìya sa-tàktub ar-risàalah hàaza as-sùbH

you will write the letter this morning
ànta sa-tàktub ar-risàalah hàaza as-sùbH

This model can be used for all forms given in this
book. (For the future of 'to be' see the entry **be**.)

Here are some examples of the future tense:

go raaH [yaròoH]

tomorrow I'll go to Baghdad
bùkra (àna) sa-aròoH ìla baghdàd

send àrsal [yùrsil]

we shall send you a telegram next week
(ìHna) sa-nùrsil ilàykum barqèeyah feel-
usbòoA al-qàadim

pay dàfa' [yàdfa']

whatever happens, we shall pay you!
Àla kul Haal, sa-nàdfa' làkum!

G

gap thàghrah
  a gap in the market thàghrah fees-sòoq

garage (*for petrol*) maнàтat banzèen

garden Hadèeqah

garlic thoom

gas (*for cooker etc.*) ghaaz

GENDER

All nouns in Arabic are either masculine or feminine. There is no neuter gender (*see also* FEMININE FORMS). In Arabic you need to know what gender a noun is so that you can make any adjectives or verbs associated with it agree – masculine or feminine.

Adjectives which describe nouns must agree in gender with those nouns:

> (*fem.*)
> **al-bìnt al-*jamèelah***
> the pretty girl
>
> (*masc.*)
> **al-wàlad az-*zakèe***
> the intelligent boy
>
> (*masc.*)
> **bayt *kabèer***
> a big house
>
> (*fem.*)
> **sayàarah *nazèefah***
> a clean car

Verbs used with a noun must agree with it in two different ways. Firstly, as you would expect, a feminine noun needs the feminine form of the verb, past or future (*see* VERBS).

> (*fem.*)
> **ash-shìrkah *dafà'at* iltizaamàat-ha**
> the company paid off its liabilities
>
> (*masc.*)
> **al-mudèer *dàfa'* al-нisàab**
> the director paid the bill
>
> (*fem.*)

al-fatòorah sa-*tàkoon* jahìzah bùkra fees-sabàaн
the invoice will be ready tomorrow morning

(*masc.*)

al-màтaar sa-*yàkoon* maqfòol bi-sàbab al-iDràab
the airport will be closed because of the strike

Secondly, and this is peculiar to Arabic, the
second person 'you' form of a verb changes, according to whether it is a man or woman being addressed
(*see* VERBS). We have already seen that there are two
forms of the pronoun 'you' – masculine and femi-
nine: **ànta** (*masc.*) and **ànti** (*fem.*) (*see also* YOU). This
applies equally to the verb form.

to a man:

hal (ànta) *turèed* finjàan qàhwah?
do you want a cup of coffee?

to a woman:

hal (ànti) *turèedee* finjàan qàhwah?
do you want a cup of coffee?

to a man:

mùmkin *taqòol* lee wayn al-mirнàaд lou samàнt?
can you tell me where the toilet is, please?

to a woman:

mùmkin *taqòolee* lee wayn as-sòoq
can you tell me where the market is, please?

to a man:

hal (ànta) *arsàlta* ar-risàalah ìla londòn?
did you send the letter to London?

to a woman:

hal (ànti) *arsàlti* ar-risàalah ìla londòn?
did you send the letter to London?

to a man:

hal *tilfànta* ìla al-maktàb?
have you phoned the office?

to a woman:

hal *tilfànti* ìla al-maktàb?
have you phoned the office?

gents (*toilet*) mirнàaд lir-rijàal رجال

get: where can I get . . .? min wayn ajèeb . . .?
   have you got . . .? Àndak . . .?
   I haven't got . . . maa Àndee . . .
   how do I get there? kayf aròoн hunàak?

how do I get to . . .? kayf aròoн ìla . . .?
will you tell me when to get off? mùmkin taqòol lee
ìmta ànzil?
we'll get back to you on that sa-natàsil beek нawl
hàaza al-mouDòoA

gift hadèeyah

GIFTS

Before you set off on your trip to the Arab world, try
to buy, say, ten small articles from your home
country – preferably with pictures of famous land-
marks that might be known to your hosts from
magazines. In the field of comestibles, this author
has yet to find a better choice than packets of
shortbread covered in pictures of kilted Scotsmen.
Shortbread is always a new experience and the kilt
provides a subject of conversation that is guaranteed
to break the ice whatever the occasion. If you are
buying something locally, chocolates and flowers are
the norm.

You don't need to take your host anything –
giving presents is not socially 'obligatory' as it is in
the West – and in any event a present should not be
large or expensive, merely symbolic. The greatest
real gift you can give, however, is praise about your
host's house and an invitation to treat him to the
delights of a meal or a day out or a visit to a cabaret
at some time in the future. A word of warning: be
careful when you are admiring the contents of your
host's house that you imply that you already have
those sorts of things at home yourself, since Arab
convention has it that any object which a guest
admires must be given to him as a present. Of course
this is not an absolutely rigid rule, but you should
bear it in mind – your host certainly will be doing so.

If you are giving a present you could say:

hàaza hadèeyah lak mìnee
this is a present to you from me

To which you will hear a variation on:

shùkran
thank you

or:

shùkran jazèelan
thank you very much

You would then complete the social exchange by replying:

　　Àfwan
　　it's nothing

girl bint
This is the origin of the British army slang 'bint' for girl. It originally found its way into the English language through the British troops stationed in the Suez Canal Zone.

give à'таа [yùатее]
　　please give me . . . lou samàнt a'тèenee . . .

glass (*for drinking*) koob
　　(*material*) zujàaj

glasses (*spectacles*) nazaaràat

gloves qufaazàat

go raaн [yaròoн]
　　tomorrow I'm going to . . . bùkra sa-aròoн li . . .
　　I went there yesterday rùнtu hunàak ams
　　where are you going? wayn taròoн?

gold zàhab

good mumtàaz
　　that's very good hàaza mumtàaz

goodbye ma' as-salàamah
　　(*more informally*) salàam

GOODBYE

ma' as-salàamah is always said by the person leaving and means literally 'in peace'. The person staying has a choice of perhaps three responses which are used according to how permanent or lengthy the separation is expected to be.

　　If the leaver is just going round the corner and will be seen again soon, the person staying will say:

　　àllah yusalìmak fee amàan ìllah

which means literally:

　　Allah protect you in the safety of Allah

If the parting is for a day or more the person staying might say:

　　fee ri'àayat àllah
　　(*literally: in the protection of Allah*)

For serious adieux when the leaver is going somewhere far away you will hear:

tawàsal bis-salàamah
may you arrive in safety

goods baDàa'iA

government Hukòomah

grateful: we're very grateful mutashakirèen

great (*tremendous*) azèem
that's really great! hàaza ràa'i bi-jàd

green àkhDar

grey ramàadee

ground arD

ground floor aT-Tàabiq al-àrDee

guarantee (*noun*) Damàan
there's a one-year guarantee fee Damàan li-mùdah sànah

guest Dayf

GUESTS

Being a guest in the Arab world should be a pleasant experience since by convention the guest never has to pay anything at all or make any arrangements. In the West even a guest can expect to offer to pay for some small things, and be allowed to, but not so in the Arab world. There the guest reigns supreme and his every whim is indulged. This can lead to embarrassment for your host and so you must be careful not to suggest or even hint that anything might be otherwise with your host's entertainment plans, however impractical or unappealing these may appear to be. If you do seem unenthusiastic your host will feel slighted and inadequate – much more so than you would do if you were acting as host in the West. The other side of the coin is that, of course, when you are the host, perhaps entertaining in your hotel or in a restaurant, your Arab guests will expect to be waited on hand and foot and will not expect to have to share the bill with you.

As a guest you should always accept at least a little of everything that is offered to you by way of food. However syrupy, strong-tasting or generally unappetizing you might find what is offered you can be sure it has been specially prepared for you and any other guests. Convention requires you to take, and eat, a small bit. On the other hand you should not show a marked preference for one particular treat either – your host will feel duty-bound to produce an inexhaustible supply of it, which may be expensive or difficult – and anyway this may lead your host to doubt your commitment to other culinary delights on offer.

The golden rule for guests is to look blissfully happy in whatever context and in reply to your host's inevitable and probably repeated questioning about your well-being say:

kùluh mumtàaz shùkran!
everything is fine, thank you!

guidebook dalèel

Gulf: the Gulf al-khalèej al-Àrabee
the Gulf States dùwal al-khalèej al-Àrabee

Note that Arabs call the Persian Gulf the Arabian Gulf.

H

hair sha'r

haircut qas ash-shà'r

hairdresser's Halàaq

half nisf
    half each kul mìna nisf
    half a kilo nisf kìlo
    half an hour nisf sà'ah
    See TIME

hand yad

handbag shànTah saghèerah

hand baggage shùnuT saghèerah

handkerchief mandèel

Almost everyone uses paper handkerchiefs in the Arab world these days – much more suitable than cloth ones in a hot climate.

HANDS – HOLDING HANDS

Strangely enough holding hands is restricted to members of the same sex in the Arab world. Two good friends, especially young people, will often hold hands in the street as a friendly gesture. This can be quite disconcerting to a Westerner, who is probably not used to seeing men holding hands in the street. Conversely if a boy and girl were to do this it might well be thought to be wantonly brazen. It must be remembered that relations between the sexes almost everywhere in the Arab world are extremely discreet and that, unless they are married, a man and woman are unlikely even to be seen walking together down the street, let alone holding hands. Usually the woman walks about four feet behind the man carrying any shopping bags or luggage they may have, leaving the man with his hands free.

happy sa'èed
    we're not happy with . . . ìHna moo su'adàa bi . . .

hard (*solid*) sulb
    (*difficult*) sà'ab

hat qùb'ah

have: I have . . . Àndee . . .
   can I have . . .? mùmkin 'aakhuz . . .?
   I don't have . . . maa Àndee . . .
   do you have . . .? (*to a man*) hal Àndak . . .?
   do you have . . .? (*to a woman*) hal Àndik . . .?
   he has . . . Ànduh . . .
   she has . . . Ànd-ha . . .
   we have . . . Andàna . . .
   they have . . . Andùhum . . .
   have they . . .? hal Andùhum . . .?
   I have to . . . làazim . . .
   I have to go tomorrow làazim aròoH bùkra
   See PAST TENSE

he hùwa

Note that the verb 'to be' is implied (in the present tense). For example:

   hùwa marèeD
   he is ill
   (*literally: he ill*)

   hùwa Tabèeb
   he is a doctor
   (*literally: he doctor*)

   hùwa abèe
   he is my father
   (*literally: he my father*)

The pronoun **hùwa** is usually omitted if the meaning is clear from the verb. If it is included, this tends to give the sentence a special emphasis. Compare these two sentences:

   did he write the report?
   hal kàtab at-taqrèer?

   did *he* write the report?
   hal hùwa kàtab at-taqrèer?

head rà'is

headache sudàa'

health sìHah
   your very good health! fee siHàtak!

hear sàmi'a [yàsma']
   I can't hear maa àsma'

heart qalb

heavy thaqèel

heel (*of foot, shoe*) kà'ab

hello àhlan
  (*on telephone*) alòo

help (*noun*) musàa'adah
  help! ìlHaq!

her (*possessive adjective*)

There are no possessive adjectives as such in Arabic; instead a suffix is added to the noun. In the case of 'her' you add **-ha** to a word ending in a consonant and **-t-ha** to feminine words ending in a vowel or **-ah** (in which case the **h** is dropped):

children	oulàad
her children	oulàad-ha
car	sayàarah
her car	sayaaràt-ha

If you use an adjective with 'her', then you must make it definite as well and prefix **al-** to the adjective:

her new car
sayaaràt-ha al-jadèedah

she left her broken suitcase at the airport
taràkat shanTàt-ha al-maksòorah feel-màTaar

her (*pronoun*)

'Her' can be either the direct object of a sentence as in 'I saw her' or it can be the indirect object as in 'I gave her the keys'.

When it is the direct object you simply add the suffix **-ha** to the verb. For example:

I saw her
àna ra'èetu-*ha*

he loved her
hùwa Habà-*ha*

we invited her to the party
ìHna da'àwna-*ha* lil-Hàflah

When 'her' is used as an indirect object you again use the suffix **-ha**, but in this case it is very often associated with a preposition:

with her	mà'ha
at her place	Ànd-ha
on her	Alàyha
to her/for her	lìha
from her	mìnha

I gave her the keys to the office
àna aтàytuha mafaatèeн al-màktab

she sold her mother her old car
bàa'at li-ùmha sayaaràt-ha al-qadèemah

Emphasis can be given by intonation:

don't give it to *her*!
laa tu'тèeha *l*ìha!

This can be made stronger by preceding it by 'by Allah' or wàllah!:

for heaven's sake, don't give it to her!
wàllah laa tu'тèeha lìha!

here hùna

hers màalha

is this yours?
hal hàaza màalak?

no, it's hers
laa hàaza màalha

don't take that, it's hers!
laa tà'khuz hàaza, hùwa màalha!

high (*hill*, *costs*) murtàfiʌ

hill tal

him

This can be either the direct object of a sentence as in 'I saw him' or it can be the indirect object as in 'I gave him some money'.

When it is the direct object you simply add the suffix **-hu** to the verb. For example:

I saw him
àna ra'èetuhu

she loved him
hìya нabàt-hu

we asked him to the meeting
ìнna da'àwnahu lil-ijtimàa'

When it is the indirect object, you again use the suffix **-hu** but in this case it is usually associated with a preposition:

with him	mà'hu
at his place	Ànd-hu
on him	Alàyhu
from him	mìnhu
to him/for him	làhu

I gave him the suitcase
àna aтàytuhu ash-shànтah

Other examples:

his colleague stayed with him in the hotel
zamèelhu bàqaa mà'hu feel-fùnduq

the steward took the tickets from him
al-muDèef àkhaz mìnhu at-tazàakir

Emphasis is given by intonation:

don't give it to him!
laa tu'тèeha *là*hu!

This can be made stronger by preceding it by 'by
Allah' or **wàllah**:

for heaven's sake, don't give it to him!
wàllah laa tu'тèeha làhu!

hire istà'jar [yastà'jir]
I want to hire a car urèed astà'jir sayàarah

his (*possessive adjective*)

There are no possessive adjectives as such in Arabic;
instead a suffix is added to the noun. In the case of
'his' you add **-hu** to a word ending in a consonant
and **-t-hu** to a word ending in a vowel or **-ah** (in
which case the **h** is dropped):

hotel	fùnduq
his hotel	fùnduqhu
company	shìrkah
his company	shirkàt-hu
car	sayaàrah
his car	sayàarat-hu

If you use an adjective with 'his' then you must
make it definite as well and prefix **al-** to the
adjective:

his old car
sayàarat-hu al-qadèemah

he has left his office
hùwa khàraj min maktàbhu

he put the money in his new wallet
wàDa' al-filoòs fee нaafizàt-hu al-jadèedah

his (*possessive pronoun*) màalah

is this mine?
hal hàaza màalee?

no, it's his
la, hùwa màalah

don't touch that, it's his!
laa tàlmis hàaza, hùwa màalah!

hole Hùfrah

holiday (*vacation, public*) ajàazah

HOLIDAYS, PUBLIC

The weekend in the Arab Muslim world is Thursday and Friday – or just Friday. Saturday and Sunday are working days except in Christian communities, such as the Egyptian Copts and the Lebanese Maronites, where the weekend is the same as in the West.

In mixed communities, each family and business take their holiday according to their religious affiliation; so in towns with a mixed Christian and Muslim population half the shops will shut on Friday and half on Sunday – handy for the consumer at least.

There is a different set of 'secular' public holidays celebrated in each country: National Day, Independence Day etc. In addition there are four important Muslim holidays which are celebrated everywhere and which produce a partial or total shut-down of business, depending where you are. Since these are linked to the Muslim (lunar) calendar (*see* CALENDAR) they fall at an earlier date each year according to the Western (solar) calendar. These four holidays are:

New Year's Day
Birth of Muhammad
Aèed al-fîTr (breaking the fast at the end of Ramadan)
Aèed al-aDHa (time for pilgrimage to Mecca – *see* RAMADAN)

home mànzil
at home feel-mànzil
the home market as-sòoq ad-daakhilèeyah

HOME

The Arabs have a great tradition of hospitality and so when you make friends with an Arab he will certainly invite you to eat out with him in a restaurant or perhaps in a cabaret or he may well invite you to his home.

If you are actually invited to someone's home you can assume the visit will include a meal – short coffee-mornings and tea-parties are held in a café (*see* CAFÉ). As you would expect there is an enormous variety of homes throughout the Arab world – as in the West. In the big cities, such as Alexandria, Cairo and Damascus, tenement blocks are the rule because of a shortage of ground space, while out in the country people of quite modest means may own a detached house with garden or orchard. To Western eyes Arab houses often look rather dilapidated and rough from the outside, but this is deceptive. In the absence of sophisticated municipal services in most areas streets are kept tidy and smart only by the inhabitants of the area. And urban streets and pavements are attended to only in cases of dire need.

Street names and numbering are very erratic and well-nigh incomprehensible even to the local residents of the large cities and you are strongly advised to get your host to write down his address in Arabic when he makes his invitation to you and then take a taxi, showing the Arabic to the driver. This author has spent literally hours unhappily trudging the dusty byways of Cairo and Damascus looking for addresses that 'could not be missed' – so be warned! There are no taxis to be had in the suburbs either, so you can get into a real mess.

You can take a small gift with you when you visit someone's home but this is not obligatory (*see* GUESTS). You should however go prepared with a well-thought-out invitation to extend to your host when you eventually leave. This *will* be expected and you should give exact details of when and where. Variations on 'well see you around soon . . .' are no good. If you don't think this out beforehand you may make a spontaneous offer which you later regret, as it will certainly be taken up.

As a man you are unlikely to meet any women when you visit an Arab's home. They will be in the kitchen or in another room away from you. Often you may hear a quiet knock at the door and your host or one of the male members of the family present will go out only to return ten seconds later with a dish of food handed to him by a woman on the other side of the door. As a woman you will have a brief and formal introduction to the men of the family and then be sent off to see the women in the kitchen or other room, since Arab men do not feel they can relax properly when there are women around. It's no good pretending that women are equal to men in the Arab world. They are not and, although attitudes are slowly changing, at the pres-

ent rate of progress it will be a very long time until
full equality for women is achieved.

hope: I hope so atamàna zàalik
I hope not laa sàmaH àllah

horrible shanèeA

hospital mustàshfa

hospitality Diyàafah
thank you for your hospitality shùkran Àla
Diyaafàtak

HOSPITALITY
Arabs are very hospitable indeed and the business
traveller will learn to be selective about accepting
offers of hospitality if he wishes to have a moment
on his own. It should be said that this hospitality
comes from the heart, not from a sense of duty, and
it is one of the great Arab traditions which has
disarmed many a hard-nosed Westerner.

If you want to decline hospitality you have two
cast-iron excuses: family matters and illness. These
two subjects are considered legitimate reasons for
declining an invitation.

Here are a few tactful phrases:

I'm sorry, but my wife is a bit unwell
àna àasif walàkin zoujàtee marèeDah shwàya

I'm sorry, but my husband is a bit unwell
àna aasìfah walàkin zòujee marèeD shwàya

I'm sorry, I have a headache (*said by a man*)
àna àasif walàkin Àndee sudàa'

I'm sorry, I have a headache (*said by a woman*)
àna aasìfah walàkin Àndee sudàa'

I'm sorry, I have indigestion (*said by a man*)
àna àasif walàkin Àndee Asr haDm

I'm sorry, I have indigestion (*said by a woman*)
àna aasìfah walàkin Àndee Asr haDm

host sàaHib ad-dà'wah

HOST
The host is the most important person at any
gathering of Arabs. It is he who sets the agenda of
where to eat, where to go and what to do. The guests
will go along with his plans for the group, whatever
they are. If you are the host – and you will be
expected to take on this role from time to time – you

will have to have a definite plan for your guests. You should also ensure that you have enough money on you to pay for things. Do not adopt the Western habit of letting your guests do their own thing and suggest their preferences. Your guests will expect you to take a firm lead in whatever you have decided. (*See* GUESTS.)

hot (*also spicy*) Haar

hotel fùnduq فندق

HOTELS
If you intend to stay in an international hotel in the Peninsula, make sure that you book in advance or you might find you have to stay in a different city.

hour sàa'ah
   in an hour fee zarf sàa'ah
   See TIME

house bayt
   See HOME

how kayf
   how do you do? kayf Hàalak?

The standard response is:

   al-Hamdulìllah
   thanks be to Allah

   how are you? kayf Hàalak?
   how long? qad aysh?
   how long does it take? (*journey etc.*) qad aysh tastàghriq?
   how many? kam?
   how much? bikàm?

humour mizàaH

HUMOUR
In general terms Arab humour is most akin to the farcical and slap-stick traditions in the West. Wearing funny clothes, funny hats, making people jump, hiding things and flummoxing people are all grist to the Arab mill. More notable perhaps are the things which are not thought at all funny by Arabs, but will in fact cause embarrassment. These include any jokes of a scatalogical nature, jokes about fat or drunken mothers-in-law, anything remotely risqué about women or any part of them and any account of salacious behaviour by anybody. Drunkenness and

lavatories are not talked about in polite Arab company and are just plain embarrassing, not funny. The
Westerner might feel that most of the traditional
butts for jokes are thus excluded and it is true to say
that Arab humour does appear to us (in Arab eyes)
decadent Westerners as 'tame' and even 'facile'
compared to what we are used to at home.

hungry jou'àan
I'm hungry àna jou'àan

If you don't want to eat something just say:

I'm not very hungry
àna moo jou'àan jìdan

and take a small piece of whatever is on offer.
Convention requires you to take a little bit of
everything you are offered even if your stomach
turns at the sight of it!

hurry: hurry! bisùr'ah!
there's no hurry Àla màhlak

hurt: it hurts tòuja'
it doesn't hurt maa tòuja'

husband zouj

HUSBANDS

Among educated Arabs both the husband and wife
go out to work. However, the very great majority of
Arabs in all Arab countries still live according to the
traditional values of working men and house-
keeping women. In Saudi Arabia and the Yemens, it
is very rare indeed to find women going out to work.
In Saudi Arabia women are not even allowed to
drive a car, so this clearly limits their freedom of
action to work even if they wished to.

It is unfortunately no use pretending that women
are equal to men in the Arab world. They are not;
the wife is seen as the husband's property, at least
among uneducated Arabs; and, of course, he can do
with his property as he pleases. The best most Arab
women can hope for is a husband who treats her
well and gives her a lot of children to look after her
in her old age. In Egypt and Lebanon women are
just beginning to make their influence felt in the
professions; but even there women are nearly always
restricted to teaching and nursing. Arab business-
women are almost completely unknown, although
there is no question that things are changing.

I

I àna

Note that the verb 'to be' is implied (in the present tense):

> **àna marèeD**
> I am ill
> (*literally: I ill*)

> **àna ràjul a'amàal**
> I am a businessman
> (*literally: I businessman*)

> **àna abùh**
> I am his father
> (*literally: I his father*)

In the past and future tenses the personal pronoun 'I' is usually omitted, since the verb says it for you. The pronoun is used, however, when you want to emphasize that it was *I* who did it and not somebody else:

> **I wrote a letter to Ahmed this morning**
> katàbtu risàalah ìla Ahmed hàaza as-sabàaH

> **he didn't write to Ahmed – I wrote to him!**
> hùwa maa kàtab ìla Ahmed – àna katàbtu ilàyhi!

ice thalj
with ice bi-thàlj

ice cream ays kreem
chocolate ice cream ays kreem shukulàatah
vanilla ice cream ays kreem vaanèela

if ìza

ill marèeD
I feel ill àshAor bi-maràD

immediately fàwran

IMPERATIVES
There are two sorts of imperative or 'ordering words': the positive as in 'go!'; 'come!'; 'stand up!' and the negative as in 'don't go!'; 'don't come!'; 'don't stand up!'.

To form the positive imperative you take the second form of the verb given in this book. For example from 'stop **tawàqaf** [yatawàqaf]' you take **tawàqaf** and make the following changes:

Singular

If speaking to one man, omit the **ya**:

> **tawàqaf!**
> stop!

If speaking to one woman, omit the **ya** and add **ee**:

> **tawàqafee!**
> stop!

Plural

If speaking to several men or women or both, omit the **ya** and add **oo**:

> **tawàqafòo!**
> stop!

Similarly for the verb 'wait **intàzar** [yantàzir]' – in this case an opening vowel is added to make the word pronounceable:

If speaking to one man:

> **intàzir!**
> wait!

If speaking to one woman:

> **intàziree!**
> wait!

If speaking to several men or women:

> **intàziroo!**
> wait!

To form a negative imperative – an order *not* to do something – you just take the future 'you' form of the verb (in this case '**tàqif** – you will stop' or '**tantàzir** – you will wait') and put **laa** (do not) before it:

> **laa tatawàqaf!**
> don't stop!

> **laa tantàzir!**
> don't wait!

Use the masculine or feminine singular or the plural according to who you are talking (or shouting!) to.

Here are all the forms of these two verbs we have been using:

> STOP
> (*to a man*)
> **laa tatawàqaf!**
> don't stop!

(*to a woman*)
laa tatawàqafee!
don't stop!

(*to several people*)
laa tatawàqafoo!
don't stop!

WAIT
(*to a man*)
laa tantàzir!
don't wait!

(*to a woman*)
laa tantàziree!
don't wait!

(*to several people*)
laa tantàziroo
don't wait

import (*verb*) istòurad [yastòurid]

important muhìm
  it is important hàaza muhìm

impossible mustaнèel

in fee
  in Egypt fee misr
  in Arabic feel-lùghah al-arabèeyah
  in my room fee ghurfàtee
  in two weeks from now fee zarf usboo'àyn min al'àn

included: is . . . included? hal . . . yashtàmil?

inflation (*economics*) taдakhùm

information ma'loomàat

information office màktab al-isti'alaamàat

instant coffee nìskafi

INSTANT COFFEE
The Arabs just use the word 'Nescafé' for this,
whatever the brand. If you want real coffee you
must ask for **qáhwah** (*see* COFFEE). Arab café-owners
usually keep a jar of powdered instant coffee handy
for tourists whose stomachs can't take any more of
the real thing – you must ask for 'Nescafé' or **nìskafi**
as Arabs pronounce it. Arabs never touch the stuff
themselves.

insurance ta'amèen

interesting mùmtiA
that's very interesting haàza mùmtiA jìdan

international dàwlee

international driving licence rùkhsat qiyàadah dawlèeyah

interpret taṙjim [yutàrjim]
could you please interpret? mùmkin tutàrjim min fàDlak?

interpreter mutàrjim
we need an interpreter naHtàaj li-mutàrjim

introduce: may I introduce . . .? mùmkin uqàdim . . .?

INTRODUCTIONS

When someone introduces you to someone they will say:

> **mùmkin uqàdim làk Mr X**
> may I introduce to you Mr X?

you reply:

> **màrHaban**
> hello

to the smiling face. You can then move on to:

> **keef Hàalak?**
> how are you?

to which the reply in most cases will be:

> **wàllah mabsòoт!**
> fine, Allah willing

introductory offer ArD tamhèedee

invitation dà'awah
thank you for the invitation shùkran Àla da'awàtak

INVITATIONS

Arabs are very hospitable and you will find yourself invited out/home/to a party by almost anyone you are introduced to. If you want to have some time alone, you will have to fall back on imaginary engagements if you are not to cause offence. Wanting to have a quiet evening is not really a plausible answer and will probably be taken as a snub. If you accept the invitation you can be sure of being spoilt, pampered and paid for if you go out (*see* GIFTS). It is normally the local person who does the inviting so if you are the visitor, either to a particular locality/house etc. or even to a country, your Arab host will invite you to events arranged by him. If you want to repay this hospitality, apart from inviting him to your home country – which may well be taken up – you can entertain him in your hotel or any big, expensive, impressive establishment. You will then pay for everything and be given presents instead.

When you have been invited you may want to accept. Then you say:

> **that's very nice of you**
> hàaza laⲧèef mìnak

or: **thanks for the invitation**
shùkran Àlad-dà'wah

If you want to decline you can say:

> **could we meet some other time?**
> mùmkin nataqàabil fee màrah ùkhrah?

or: **I'm very sorry but I'm already invited for this evening**
àna àasif jìdan walàkin àna Àndee Aʐòomah hàaza al-masàa

invite dà'a [yàdAoo]
can I invite you out for a meal? mùmkin àdAook li-wàjbat ghazàa?
See INVITATIONS

invoice (*noun*) faatòorah [(*pl*) fawàatir]

Iraq 'iràaq

Iraqi (*adjective, noun*) 'iràaqee

Ireland irlànda

Irish irlàndee

iron (*for clothes*) màkwah
(*material*) Hadèed
could you please get these ironed? mùmkin tàkwee hàazil aghràaD?

is *see* **be**

island jazèerah

Israel israa'èel

ISRAEL

Most Arabs feel strongly about Israel in a negative way but realize at the same time that many Westerners are ambivalent or feel sympathetic about that country. Israel is the one subject which is guaranteed to sour a pleasant meeting and take the warmth out of a cosy chat. Nothing a Westerner can say can dispel the feeling among Arabs that it was the West, and especially Britain and America, that brought Israel into existence. Consequently Westerners, particularly British and American visitors, should treat the subject of Israel and all its works as taboo and decline to be drawn into a discussion at any cost.

Israeli (*adjective, noun*) israa'èelee

it

The Arabic words for 'it' in many cases is **hùwa**, which literally means 'he'. If the 'it' is patently feminine (*see* FEMININE FORMS) you use **hìya**, which literally means 'she'. Note that, in Arabic, place names, cities and rivers are feminine. Here are some examples:

> **is Cairo beautiful? – yes it is very beautiful**
> hal al-qaahìrah jamèelah? – àywa, hìya jamèelah jìdan
>
> **it's big**
> hùwa kabèer
>
> **is it far?**
> hal hùwa ba'èed
>
> **it's yours**
> hùwa màalak
>
> **it's mine**
> hùwa màalee

When you are talking about the weather instead of **hùwa** for 'it' you use the noun **al-jòu** (the weather):

> **it is hot!**
> al-jòu Haar!
>
> **it is cold!**
> al-jòu bàarid!

J

jacket jaakèet
  See CLOTHING

jam *(for bread)* muràba

January yanàayeer

jetlag: I'm/he's suffering from jetlag àna/hùwa ta'abàan min ta'athèer as-sàfar

jewellery mujouharàat

job *(work)* shughl
  what's your job? aysh tashtàghil?
  (order) Tàlab
  if we get this job ìdha ràsat Alàyna hàaza aT-Tàlab

joint venture mashròoA mushtàrak

joke *(noun)* nùktah
  you're joking! bijàd!, saнèeн!

Jordan al-'urdùn

Jordanian *(adjective, noun)* 'urdùnee

journey rìнlah
  safe journey! rìнlah sa'èedah

July yòoleeyoo

June yòoneeyoo

just *(only)* fàqaт
  just one *(masc.)* wàнid fàqaт
  (fem.) waнìdah fàqaт
  just a little bit qìт'ah saghèerah fàqaт

K

keep: please keep it iHtàfiz bìha
keep the change khàlee al-bàaqee

key miftàaн [(*pl*) mafaatèeн]
the key for room . . . miftàaн al-ghùrfah . . .

kilo kìloo

kilometre kìloomitr

kind: that's very kind of you hàaza karàm mìnak
what kind of . . .? aysh nòuA . . .?

king màlik

kiss (*noun*) bòosah

KISSING

If an Arab has not seen a friend of the same sex for a
long time, they will often shake hands and then kiss
each other on the cheek. If the friend is of the
opposite sex or a relative then they will only shake
hands – just the opposite of what is normal in the
West!

On your second business trip you will almost
certainly be kissed by your host and any other men
you know from the first time round. A word of
warning: do not follow the Western practice of
kissing your hostess, however many times you may
have seen her – which may be never anyway!
Women in the Arab world are kissed by their
husbands in private and no one else.

kitchen màтbakh

knee rùkbah

knife sikèen [(*pl*) sakaakèen]
can I have a knife and fork, please? mùmkin
ta'aтèenee sikèen wa shòukah lou samàнt?

know Àraf [yà'rif]
I don't know maa Àa'rif
I know him àna Aa'rìfuh
I don't know him àna maa Aa'rìfuh
I didn't know that maa Àaref zàalik
I knew him Aarèfhu
do you know where . . .? hal tà'rif wayn . . .?

Koran Qur'àan

Kuwait koowàyt

Kuwaiti (*adjective, noun*) koowàytee

L

ladies (*toilet*) mirHàaD as-sayidàat سيدات

lady sayìdah

lamb Dàanee

lane (*narrow street*) zuqàaq

language lùghah

LANGUAGE

There are basically three different kinds of Arabic language: classical or Koranic Arabic, Standard Literary Arabic and Spoken Arabic.

Classical or Koranic Arabic, as its name suggests, is the Arabic which the Koran was written in (around 632 A D) as well as the subsequent commentaries and homilies on it which were written during the Middle Ages. It has an ornate, flowery style in keeping with the visual arts associated with it. It is a delight to read and not particularly difficult but is in a complex form of Arabic not used in everyday life. Arabic purists insist classical Arabic is the 'true Arabic'. Anyway it was certainly the first Arabic to be written down.

Standard Literary Arabic is the written Arabic language which has developed since the Middle Ages, and especially since the advent of Arabic printing-presses in the later nineteenth century. It is the Arabic used in newspapers all over the Arab world. From Morocco to Iraq the Standard Literary Arabic is universally understood by educated Arabs. If this Arabic is read out loud you get a rather stilted and formal form of Arabic – a bit like reading a Court Order or an Act of Parliament out loud in English. However stilted, it has the major advantage of being understood by educated Arabs anywhere in the Arab world. This is the language of radio broadcasts – including the B B C World Service – and because of the need for Arab governments to reach Arab audiences in many other, often hostile and distant states even greater standardization has come about through the frequent use of common words at the expense of regional ones. The radio announcer who has just read out a broadcast in this Standard Literary Arabic will switch into quite a

different sort of Arabic when he is off the air and
shouting at the studio technicians – Spoken Arabic.

There are about as many forms of Spoken Arabic
as there are Arab states – some twenty. Broadly
speaking however Spoken Arabic can be divided into
three groups. 'Gulf Arabic' is the Arabic spoken in
Saudi Arabia, Iraq, Kuwait, Bahrain, Qatar, the Arab
Emirates, Oman and the Yemens; 'Palestinian Arabic' is the Arabic spoken in Syria, Lebanon, Palestine and Jordan; while Egypt has a dialect of its own.
'North African' Arabic is spoken in Libya, Tunisia,
Algeria and Morocco. Of course there is some
overlapping of groups – and Egypt, for example, has
many words only used in Egypt. However, within
these groups the spoken language is mutually intelli-
gible – but this often does not hold true outside the
group. When a Moroccan businessman wants to talk
to an Omani, for example, they will both have to
speak Standard Literary Arabic to understand each
other. It may surprise you to learn that, at large Arab
conferences, Arabs often use English or French to
converse with each other informally – sometimes
with Arabic words thrown in – since this is easier for
them than putting all their thoughts into Standard
Literary Arabic! You could call this mixture the
language of educated Arabs.

This book tries, as every language book does, to
have the best of both worlds. The Arabic you are
learning in this book is a blend of Standard Literary
Arabic and the most common words used everywhere in Spoken Arabic. If you master the main
points of this book you will be genuinely surprised at
the ability you will have gained to make yourself
understood in the Arab world. If it also gives you a
taste for further study of one of the world's great
languages it will certainly have served its purpose
well.

large kabèer

last (*latest, last in series*) akhèer
  last week al-usbòoA al-màaDee
  last night al-làylah al-maaDèeyah
  last year as-sànah al-maaDèeyah
  the last time we met akhèer màrah taqaabàlna

late muta'àkhar
  sorry for being late àasif Alat-ta'akhèer
  delivery will be two weeks late at-taslèem sa-
  yata'àkhar usboo'àyn

later ba'adèen
I'll come back later sa-àrja' màrah thaanèeyah ba'adèen

laugh (*verb*) DàHak [yàDHak]

laundry màghsalah

law qaanòon [(*pl*) qawaanèen]

lawyer muHàamee

learn ta'àlam [yata'àlam]
I'd like to learn Arabic urèed ata'àlam Arabèe

leave (*depart, general sense*) ghàadar [yughàadir]
(*travel*) sàafar [yusàafir]
I'm leaving in the morning àna musàafir feeS-SabàaH
when does the plane leave? ìmta taTèer aT-Tayàarah?

Lebanese (*adjective, noun*) lubnàanee

Lebanon lubnàan

left yasàar
on the left Àlal-yasàar

LEFT HAND
In the Arab world the left hand is regarded as unclean and should not be used for eating or drinking. You will notice that many Arabs keep their left hand out of sight behind their back when they are eating or drinking. If you are left-handed you should perhaps remember the reaction that using your left hand will cause and make an effort to use the right.

left luggage (office) al-amaanàat

leg rijl

less àqal
less than a year àqal min sànah

letter (*mail*) khiTàab

letter of credit khiTàab iAtimàad

letterbox sùndooq barèed صندوق البريد

LETTERS
Letters are not often written in English, mainly because typewriters with a Roman typeface are rare in Arab countries. When they are written in English

they try to imitate the English or American model as closely as possible.

Libya lèebiya

Libyan (*adjective*, *noun*) lèebee

lift (*elevator*) mìs'ad

light (*electric light*) noor
(*not dark*) fàatiн
(*not heavy*) khafèef
do you have a light? hal ʌndak kibrèet?
the light's not working an-nòor maqтòoʌ

like: I'd like a ... urèed ...
would you like a ...? (*to a man*) hal turèed ...?
(*to a woman*) hal turèedee ...?
I like it ya'ajìbnee
I don't like it maa ya'ajìbnee
she likes it ya'ajìbha
he doesn't like it maa ya'ajìbhuh
like this mithl hàaza

litre litr

little (*small*) saghèer
a little qalèel
a little sugar mal'àqat sùkar

live sàkan [yàskun]
I live in ... àna àskun fee ...

loan words kalimàat musta'àarah

LOAN WORDS
Most pieces of equipment or machinery imported from the West retain their original name, as do drinks and parts of the car. For example: 'brandy', 'gin', 'whisky', 'clutch', 'steering'. Like the French, Arab governments periodically try to clean up their language and eliminate loan words by introducing Arabic neologisms.

lock (*on door*) qifl
it's locked hùwa maqfòol
excuse me, I'm locked out min fàdlak, àna nasàyt al-miftàaн bid-dàakhil

London londòn

long тawèel
a long time mùdah тawèelah

look: can I have a look? mùmkin ànzur?
    I'm just looking, thanks shùkran, àna atafàraj fàqaт
    that looks good hàaza shàkluh jamèel
    I look forward to meeting you again atamàna uqaabìlak màrah thaanèeyah

look! shouf!

lorry shaaHìnah

lose fàqad [yàfqud]
    I've lost my ... faqàdatu ...
    I'm lost, can you help me? mùmkin tusaa'ìdnee – àna tàayih

lot: a lot of ... kathèer min ...
    a lot kathèer
    a lot better àHsan bi-kathèer
    not a lot moo kathèer

love (*noun*) Hub
    I love you (*to a woman*) uHìbik
    (*to a man*) uHìbak

lovely (*stay*, *day*, *view*) jamèel

low (*prices*) munkhàfiD

luck HaZ
    good luck! HaZ sa'èed!

luggage aghràaD
    my luggage aghràaDee

lunch ghazàa

LUNCH

Lunch is served between 1.30 and 3 p.m. in the Arab world – both in private homes and in restaurants. Most jobs in government, schools and offices start at 8 a.m., or even earlier, and run through to 1.30 or 2 p.m. When workers get home, or to their favourite restaurant, they feel like eating a large meal – the main meal of the day – lunch.

    Lunch at home or in a restaurant will consist of an opening course, a main course and a dessert. The opening course is usually various plates of salad and spicy bite-size nibbles designed to whet the appetite rather than assuage it. Then comes the main course, which is always hot and accompanied by a generous helping of 'padding' – either rice, potatoes, pasta, couscous or some kind of pulse-stew. Desserts tend to come in individual portions rather than dollops out of a main dish and are often too sweet for many a Westerner's palate.

It may seem odd in such a hot climate as exists in much of the Arab world for most of the time that the main meal should be eaten at lunch-time. From the Arabs' point of view, however, it is then that the work of the day is done and the very hot mid-afternoon can be spent drowsing happily in the shade with a full stomach – an activity few Westerners would decline given the opportunity! If you have eaten out you will retire to a shady coffee-house and drink enough coffee to ward off a public display of somnolence.

M

machine maakèenah

mad majnòon

mail (*noun: letters*) barèed
   we'll mail it sa-nursìlha bil-barèed

make (*general word*) sàwee [yusàwee]
   (*manufacture*) sàna' [yàsna']
   our company make these shirkàtna tàsna' hàazee

man ràjul [(*pl*) rijàal]
   the men who . . . ar-rijàal ìllee . . .

management (*people*) idàarah
   our management idaaràtna
   your management idaaràtkum

manager (*of restaurant, hotel, business etc.*) mudèer [(*pl*)
   mudaràa]

managing director mudèer mubaàshir

manners aadàab
   good manners aadàab Hamèedah
   bad manners qìlat al-aadàab

MANNERS
Compared to most Westerners, Arabs have impec-
cable manners and are very solicitous of their
Western colleagues' comfort and well-being at all
times. On your visit to the Arab world you will find
yourself showered with gifts, offers of evenings out
and other entertainments of many kinds; and these
offers will be genuinely made – not just as a matter
of form. Good manners will dictate that you accept
these offers at face value – or decline with a
plausible reason – and not prevaricate wondering if
the offer is meant to be accepted or not. While it is
very nice for you to be at the receiving end of
invitations you must play your part as well: 'good
manners' means that you should *always* return an
invitation or gift which is extended to you as soon as
you practically can. Many Western businessmen see
a foreign trip as a good way of being entertained and
generally pampered without too much being asked
in return, but this won't do in the Arab world! You
should go armed with small gifts (*see* GIFTS) and

before you start your business try to locate a few smart restaurants near your hotel so that you can take the initiative and invite someone out on the spur of the moment. No Arab is going to be offended if, when he has just invited you to his favourite night-club, you rejoin with a firm invitation to *your* 'local' watering-hole.

As far as personal manners are concerned bear in mind that your Arab colleague will be trying to 'act the Westerner' as far as possible and you should not come across any unusual or alarming behaviour regarding manners. Make sure you conform to your host's ideal of Western manners though: no nose-picking at meetings, coughing at your host or yawning at your business-partner.

many kathèer
  not many taxis maa fee takseeyàat kathèerah

map kharèetah
  I'd like a map of ... urèed kharèeтah li ...

March maars

market (*also for business*) sooq [(*pl*) aswàaq]

MARRIAGE

It is fair to say that the very great majority of Arabs get married and have children – far more so than in the West. This is mainly because of the way Arab society treats relationships between the sexes. In the absence of almost any promiscuity at all the only way an Arab can have a sex life of any seriousness is to get married.

In Islamic law a man may marry up to four women, but he must be able to support them all and treat them equally. The financial burden of more than one spouse precludes most Arabs from even contemplating polygamy, but it is still practised especially in Saudi Arabia, the Yemens and the Gulf States.

The Western concept of being a bachelor or spinster by choice is really something Arabs cannot understand and most suspect that frigidity or perversion must lie behind this attitude.

married (*man*) mutazàwij
  (*woman*) mutazawìjah
  I'm married àna mutazàwij/mutazawìjah

marvellous badèeA

matches kibrèet

matter: it doesn't matter moo muhìm

mattress martàbah

MATTRESSES
The most common form of bed in the Arab world is
a mattress which is unrolled onto the floor of one of
the rooms of the house at night which then becomes
the bedroom. Rolled-up mattresses are thus a common sight in many households, especially in the
Gulf region.

maximum (*noun*) al-àqsa

May màayoo

may: may I ...? mùmkín ...?
may I have ... please? mùmkin ... lou samàHt?

maybe min al-mùmkin

me
This can be either the direct object of the sentence
as in 'the policeman hit me' or the indirect object as
in 'he gave me some money'.
When it is the direct object you simply add the
suffix **-nee** to the verb. For example:
(**hit**: Dàrab/yàDrub)

> **the policeman hit me**
> ash-shùrTee DaràbnEe

(**invite**: dà'a/yàdAoo)

> **the manager invited me to his house**
> al-mudèer da'ànee ìla bàyt-hu

When 'me' is the indirect object of the sentence
you will find it can usually be translated as 'to me',
although we often omit the 'to' in English. For
example:
(**give**: à'Taa/yùATee)

> **he gave me an invoice for the goods**
> hùwa a'Tàanee fatòorah lil-biDàa'i

(**pay**: dàfa'/yàdfuA)

> **he paid me in cash**
> hùwa dafà'lee nàqdan

Some other translations of 'me' with prepositions are:

for me	lee
to me	lee
with me	mà'ee

buy it for me
ishtaràahu lee

you can have confidence in me
mùmkin tàthiq fèeya

I haven't got it on me
hùwa maa mà'ee
(*literally: it isn't with me*)

he sat behind me
hùwa jàlas waràa'ee

come with me!
ta'aal mà'ee!

give me the key
ATèenee al-miftàaH

meal wàjbah
that was an excellent meal kàanat wàjbah mumtàzah

MEALS

Three meals are taken in the Arab world. Breakfast (**fiTòor**) as taken in the Arab world is a substantial meal of eggs, white cheese, beans and fruit and is often eaten before 7 a.m. It must be substantial since it has to see the eater through the morning's work – often the work of the day – until lunch (**ghazàa**).

Lunch is the main meal of the day with plenty of pasta, rice or potatoes. In Algeria and Morocco the pasta or rice or potatoes will be replaced with couscous (*see* FOOD). After a siesta and possibly a further stint of work in the early evening it will be time for dinner (**Ashàa**).

Dinner is a light meal, often eaten out with friends, and is taken late by Western standards: from 8 to 11 p.m. You will usually be able to find a meal after midnight in the big cities and with all the street-side snackbars which are open all day you will always be able to get something to eat if a meal doesn't materialize when you had expected it.
See also BREAKFAST, DINNER, LUNCH

mean: what does this sign mean? shoo mà'na hàazil-Alàamah?

meat laHm لَحم

Mecca màkka

MECCA

Mecca is the religious capital of the Muslim world and, whenever Muslims pray, they turn towards Mecca to do so. To travel in pilgrimage to Mecca at least once in a lifetime is a religious obligation on Muslims who have the means to do so. The Holy Mosque (*see* MOSQUE) is situated at Mecca and, during the month of pilgrimage, **zu al-Hijah**, the population of the city swells from some 200,000 to over 2 million.

medicine dawàa' [(*pl*) adwèeyah]

Mediterranean Sea al-bàHr al-mutawàsiT

meet: pleased to meet you (*said by man*) àna sa'èed bi-muqaabalàtak
(*said by woman*) àna sa'èedah bi-muqaabalàtak

meeting ijtimàa'
shall we arrange another meeting? mùmkin nuràtib ijtimàa' thàanee?

MEETING PEOPLE

When you are first introduced to someone in a formal setting, perhaps at a business gathering or a party, there is a short exchange of dialogue which is always adhered to. The person introducing you to someone says:

> **can I introduce you to my friend, Mr Haidar?**
> mùmkin uqadìmlak sadèeqee as-sàyid Haidar?

Or: **can I introduce you to my colleague, Mr Fouzi?**
> mùmkin uqadìmlak zamèelee as-sàyid Fouzi?

To which the third party, the person being introduced, says:

> **as-salàam Alàykum!**
> peace be upon you!

The reply to this is:

> **Alàykum as-salàam!**
> upon you be peace!

In a more informal setting, perhaps in the street or in a café, the introducer says the same as before:

> **can I introduce my friend, Ali al-Kharash?**
> mùmkin uqadìmlak sadèeqee Ali al-Kharash?

The third party says:

àhlan wa sàhlan
welcome

And the reply is:

àhlan beek
welcome to you

Plain 'hello!' or 'hi!' to your pal in the street is:

àhlan!
hi and welcome!

And the reply is:

àhlan beek!
hi and welcome to you!

Some other useful phrases you will want when meeting people are:

please sit down
tafàDal istaràayaH

how are you?
kayf Hàalak?

very well thanks and you?
al-Hàmdu lìllah wa kayf Hàalak ànta?

If you need to get away quickly you can always fall back on:

please excuse me, I have an appointment
ismàH lee, Àndee mee'àad

mention: don't mention it! (*said when someone thanks you for a favour*) laa shukr Àla-wàajib!
(*said when someone bumps into you and apologizes*)
Àfwan!

menu qàa'imat aт-тà'aam
the menu please qaa'ìmat aт-тà'aam lou samàHt
See FOOD

message risàalah
can I leave a message? mùmkin àtruk risàalah?
can I leave a message for ...? mùmkin àtruk risàalah li ...?

This Arabic word for 'message' is also another name for the Koran; Muhammad is the **rasòol** – the messenger.

metre mitr

This Arabic word is usually used in the singular, although you may hear the plural **amtàar**.

middle (*noun*) wàsaт
    (*adjective*) mutawàsiт

Middle East ash-shàrq al-àwsaт

midnight nisf al-làyl

mile meel
    This Arabic word is usually used in the singular, although you may hear the plural **amyàal**.

milk Halèeb حليب

mine màalee

    is that suitcase mine?
    hal hàazee ash-shànтah màalee?

    no, it belongs to that lady
    la, hìya maal tìlka as-sayìdah

mineral water miyàah ma'adanèeyah

minimum (*noun*) al-àqal

minute daqèeqah [(*pl*) daqàa'iq]
    just a minute daqèeqah waHìdah lou samàнt

mirror meeràayah

Miss àanisah
    Miss! (*to waitress etc.*) lou samàнtee!

MISS
There is no equivalent to the English 'Miss' as used to a waitress or school-teacher. In the classroom children say **ya ustàazah** – teacher.

mistake ghàlтah

MISTAKES
If you behave in a normal, courteous and reasonable manner you will not make any behavioural mistakes on your trip to the Arab world.

The only mistakes you are likely to make concern subjects of conversation. You will come to no harm if you steer clear of discussion of: religion and politics, women, Israel, bodily functions and sex of any kind. Also pigs and pork are taboo. Even if your opinion is solicited on any of these subjects be very cautious indeed in expressing criticism and especially approbation. *See also* LEFT HAND.

modern Hadèeth

Monday youum al-ithnàyn

money filòos   مال

MONEY
The only thing which the monetary systems of all
Arab countries have in common is that they are all
decimal. Each country has its own currency system
and regulations, sometimes including exchange control regulations. There is always one main unit of
currency, which is divided into 100 or sometimes
1,000 smaller units. As you can see below, although
the pound and dinar are common to several countries their actual value is totally different in each
case. All banks quote a rate in local currency for the
U S dollar, so the dollar is the best universal
yardstick for measuring the real cost of things
locally. In Arabic the unit of currency is usually left
in the singular.

Here is a list of the currencies used in Arab
countries:

Algeria	1 dinar	=	100 centimes
Bahrain	1 dinar	=	1,000 fils
Egypt	1 pound	=	100 piastres
the Emirates	1 dirham	=	100 fils
Iraq	1 dinar	=	1,000 fils
Jordan	1 dinar	=	1,000 fils
Kuwait	1 dinar	=	1,000 fils
Lebanon	1 pound	=	100 piastres
Libya	1 dinar	=	1,000 dirhams
Mauritania	1 ouguiya	=	5 khoums
Morocco	1 dirham	=	100 centimes
North Yemen	1 riyal	=	100 fils
Oman	1 riyal	=	1,000 baisa
Qatar	1 riyal	=	100 dirhams
Saudi Arabia	1 riyal	=	100 halalas
Somalia	1 shilin	=	100 cents
South Yemen	1 dinar	=	1,000 fils
Sudan	1 pound	=	100 piastres
Syria	1 pound	=	100 piastres
Tunisia	1 dinar	=	1,000 millimes

Remember, each and every one has a different
value.

Now some expressions:

I bought it for 30 riyals
àna ishtaràituhu bi-thalaathèen riyàal

he sold it to me for 6 dinars and 300 fils
hùwa ba'àha lee bi-sìtah dìnar wa thalàath
mèeyah fils

it cost me 90 dirhams
hùwa kalàfnee tisʌèen dìrham

I want some small change, please
àna urèed bà'ᴀD al-fìkah, lou samàHt

not large notes, please
maa urèed awràaq min fì'ah kabèerah lou
samàHt

And also some idiomatic expressions:

that meal cost a small fortune
tìlka al-wàjbah kalàfat màblaghan Dùkhman

we got our money's worth on that excursion
ìHna akhàzna bi-Hàqna fee tìlka an-nùzha

he's in the money
hùwa àsbaH ghanèe

month shahr [(pl) shuhòor]

MONTHS
These are the names of the months in Arabic. The
Gregorian calendar is used for all business arrange-
ments. You will see that the Arabic is just really the
Arab way of pronouncing the English names of the
months:

January	yanàayeer
February	fibràayeer
March	maars
April	ibrèel
May	màayoo
June	yòoneeyoo
July	yòoleeyoo
August	aghùsTus
September	siptìmbir
October	octùbar
November	noofìmbir
December	deesìmbir

And some phrases using names of months:

I am going to Baghdad next month
sa-aròoH ìla-baghdàd ash-shàhr al-qàadim

we were in Kuwait six months ago
kùna feel-kuwàit qabl sìtah shuhòor

they paid us last month
dàfʌoo làna ash-shàhr al-màaDee

we have been here since May
ìHna kùna hùna mùnzu shahr màayoo

The Arabic lunar calendar is used only for legal and
religious matters. It has twelve months of twenty-
nine and thirty days alternately, totalling 354 days, so
the Muslim calendar years pass more quickly than
the Christian ones. The Muslim New Year falls
earlier and earlier each Christian year. The Muslim
era dates from 622 A D, which is the date of
Muhammad's flight from Mecca.

Here are the names of the twelve Muslim months
so you will recognize them if you come across them:

1. muHàram
2. sàfar
3. rabèeA al-àwal
4. rabèeA al-àakhir
5. jumàada al-òolah
6. jumàada al-aakhìrah
7. ràjab
8. sha'abàan
9. ramaDàan (see RAMADAN)
10. shawàal
11. zu al-qà'adah
12. zu al-Hìjah

moon al-qàmar

more àkthar
  no more, thanks shùkran kifàayah
  could I have some more? mùmkin shiwàyah kàman
  lou samàHt?
  more than 100 àkthar min mìyah
  See COMPARISON OF ADJECTIVES

morning sabàaH
  in the morning fees-sabàaH
  tomorrow morning bùkrah fees-sabàaH
  this morning hàaza as-sabàaH
  good morning sabàaH al-khàyr

Moroccan màghribee

Morocco al-màghrib

Moslem (*noun*) mùslim
  (*adjective*) mùslim

mosque màsjid

MOSQUES

However small an Arab village may be, you can be sure it will boast at least two communal institutions: a coffee-house and a mosque. Large cities may have over a hundred mosques spread out so that one is accessible for every neighbourhood – rich and poor, commercial and residential.

While many Muslims go to the mosque up to five times a day to say their prayers, others may say them at home and attend the mosque only on Fridays, the Muslim day of rest, to take part in a large communal act of worship.

The worshippers always face Mecca when they pray in a mosque and there is no fixed hierarchy of priests, as there is in the Christian church. Any Muslim may lead other Muslims in worship. Of course there are many Muslim clerics who are well-versed in the Koranic traditions and who are often attached to a particular mosque. But their status is that of respected academic rather than a sanctified priest.

The most famous mosque in the world is the Holy Mosque in Mecca. This is the centre of pilgrimage for Muslims everywhere, especially during the Muslim month of pilgrimage – **zu al-Hìjah** (the pilgrimage itself being called the **Haaj**). This mosque can accommodate over a quarter of a million souls. Within its walls is contained the **kà'aba**, which is a holy black rock housed in an ornate casing. It is revered by every Muslim and, according to Muslim tradition, it dates back to the days of Abraham or even Adam. You could say it is the centre of the Muslim world.

most: most of them aghlabeeyàt-hum

mother um

motor mootòor

motorcycle mootoosèekl

mountain jàbal [(*pl*) jibàal]

moustache shàarib

mouth fam

Mr as-sàyid [**Messrs** as-sàadah]

Mrs as-sayìdah

MR & MRS

You use these two titles before the family name of a person when you are describing them to a third party:

> **I said to Mr al-Baz ...**
> qùltu ìlas-sàyid al-Baz ...

> **I went with Mrs al-Yaldani**
> rìHtu mà'as-sayìdah al-Yaldani

When you address people directly you say:

> **Mr al-Baz, hello!**
> ya sàyid al-Baz!

> **Mrs al-Yaldani, hello!**
> ya sayìdah al-Yaldani!

much: much bigger àkbar bi-kathèer
  much faster àsra' bi-kathèer
  there's not much left maa fee kathèer bàaqee

music moosèeqa

Muslim (*noun*) mùslim
  (*adjective*) mùslim

must: must I ...? làazim à...?
  must we ...? làazim nà...?
  I must ... làazim à...
  we must làazim nà...

my

There are no possessive adjectives as such in Arabic; instead a suffix is added to the word. In the case of 'my' you add -ee to a word ending in a consonant and -tee to a word ending in a vowel or -ah (in which case the h is dropped). For example:

> **parents**
> waalidàyn

> **my parents**
> waalidàynee

> **apartment**
> shàqah

> **my apartment**
> shàqatee

If you use an adjective with 'my', then you must make it definite and add al- to the adjective:

> **my English newspaper**
> jareedàtee al-ingleezèeyah

> **my first meeting**
> ijtimàa'ee al-àwal

N

nail clippers asàafat azàafir

nail scissors maqàs azàafir

name ism [(*pl*) asmàa']
  my name is . . . ìsmee . . .
  what's your name? shoo ìsmak?
  what's his name? shoo ìsmuh?
  what's her name? shoo ismàha?
  what's the name of the hotel? shoo ism al-fùnduq?

NAMES

When you are dealing with Arab personal names it is best to disregard ideas of Christian names and surnames and think instead of first names and family names. Apart from anything else, a Muslim may be offended if you start talking about Christian names.

The family name often begins with **al-**, for example **al-Baz**, **al-Yaldani**. The first name will be something like **Abdullah**, **Muhammad**, **Abdul-Aziz**, **Abdul-Rahman**, **Hussein**, **Hassan**, **Ali** or **Osman**.

When you first meet someone you would address them as **ya sàyid al-Yaldàni** or **ya sàyid al-Baz** using just the family name and **as-sàyid** (Mr). If the person has a very high status – a judge, a minister, a general, for example – you would continue to use this formula during a meeting.

Business colleagues and friends will immediately tell you their first name and call you by yours. This is not considered over-familiar as it might be in the West and you would then be on **ya Hussein!** and **ya Jeremy!** terms from the outset of your relationship.

The family name is normally used only between friends to differentiate between several people called Hussein or Muhammad etc.

napkin fòoTat al-maa'ìdah

NAPKINS

Since a lot of meals are eaten with a minimum of cutlery you will always find napkins – paper ones not cloth – provided whenever you sit down to eat anywhere. Since moustaches are grown by most Arab men napkins are a very important element in

any meal involving sauces, crumbs or stickiness of
any kind!

nationality jinsèeyah

natural (*flavour*, *taste*) Tabèe'ee

near qarèeb
    is it near here? hal hìya qarèeb min hùna?
    is it near Baghdad? hal hìya qarèeb min baghdàd?
    do you stop near ...? hal toùqaf qarèeb min ...?
    the nearest ... àqrab ...
    where is the nearest ...? wayn àqrab ...?

necessary Daròoree

neck raqàbah

need: I need ... aнtàaj ...
    do you need ...? hal taнtàaj ...?

needle ìbrah
    needle and thread ìbrah wa fàtlah

NEGATIVES

In Arabic the way of forming the negative varies
according to whether the verb you want to make
negative is in the past, future or present tense.

In the *present tense* you put the word **moo** before
the verb you want to negate. For example:

    I am writing a letter
    àna ba-àktub risàalah

    I am not writing a letter
    àna maa ba-àktub risàalah

In the present tense the Arabic verb is often omitted.
For example:

    I am tired
    àna ta'abàan

which means literally:

    I tired

In such cases the negative word **moo** is placed where
a verb would be. For example:

    I am not tired
    àna moo ta'abàan

    the shop is closed
    ad-dukàan maqfòol

    the shop is not closed
    ad-dukàan moo maqfòol

she is the manageress
hìya al-mudèerah

she isn't the manageress
hìya moo al-mudèerah

In the *past tense* you put the word **maa** before the verb which you want to negate. For example:

I was late for the meeting
àna kùntu muta'àkhir An al-ijtimàa'

I wasn't late for the meeting
àna maa kùntu muta'àkhir An al-ijtimàa'

he dismissed the man responsible for the problem
hùwa ràfat ar-ràjul al-mas'òol An al-mushkìlah

he didn't dismiss the man responsible for the problem
hùwa maa ràfat ar-ràjul al-mas'òol An al-mushkìlah

he had shares in the company
kaan Ànduh as-hàam feesh-shìrkah

he didn't have shares in the company
maa kaan Ànduh as-hàam feesh-shìrkah

I was very hungry
àna kùntu jou'àan jìdan

I wasn't very hungry
àna maa kùntu jou'àan jìdan

In the *future tense* you have a choice of negatives. To make a general negative you again put **maa** before the verb which you want to negate.

For example:

I shall go there again
sa-'aròoH hunàak màrah thaanèeyah

I shan't go there again
maa sa'aròoH hunàak màrah thaanèeyah

we shall meet next week in London
sa-nataqàabil al-usbòoA al-qàadim fee londòn

we shan't meet next week in London
maa sa'nataqàabil feel-usbòoA al-qàadim fee londòn

To make the negative more emphatic you can use **lan** instead of **maa**. The implication with **lan** is 'never' or 'extremely unlikely'. Compare the two negatives below:

he will pay you next month
sa-yàdfa'lak feesh-shàhr al-qàadim

he won't pay you next month
maa sa-yàdfa'lak feesh-shàhr al-qàadim

But: **he'll never pay you next month!**
lan yàdfa'lak feesh-shàhr al qàadim!

Or: **we shall sign the contract tomorrow**
sa-nuwàqiA Àlal-Aqd bùkra

But: lan nuwàqiA Àlal-Aqd

could be translated as:

we're never likely to sign that sort of contract

negotiations mufaawaDàat

neither: which one? – neither ay wàaHid? – walà
neither do I walà àna

nervous (*anxious*) qàliq
(*fearful*) khàa'if

net price as-sìAr as-sàafee

never àbadan

new jadèed

New Year ra's as-sànah

NEW YEAR
New Year is 1 January of the Christian calendar and
is taken as a public holiday in most Arab countries.
The Muslim calendar has its own New Year, which
falls at a different time each year (according to the
Christian calendar and the seasons) and this is a
public holiday in all Arab countries. It falls, of
course, on the first of the first Muslim month –
muHàram (*see* MONTHS) – and for the three years
following the date of writing: 4 August 1989; 24 July
1990; 13 July 1991.

New Zealand neeòozeelàandah

news (*on TV etc.*) akhbàar
is there any news? fee ay akhbàar?

newspaper jarèedah [(*pl*) jaràayid] جريدة
English newspapers jaràayid ingleezèeyah

next (*coming*) al-jàay
next year as-sànah al-jaàyah
at the next bus stop fee mòuqif al-basàat al-jaàyah
next to janb
next to the hotel janb al-fùnduq

nice (*person, meal, day*) laTèef
    that's very nice of you hàaza laTèef mìnak

night layl
    good night (*going to bed*) tìsbaH Àla khayr

    Literally this means 'get through to the morning well'.

Nile nahr an-nèel

no laa
    there's no toilet paper maa fee wàraq toowaalèet
    I have no ... maa Àndee ...

NO

If you want to say no to an offer of yet another cup of coffee or sticky bun rather than just say **laa**, which is a bit abrupt, you can say:

    laa shùkran
or: **laa mutashàkir**
    thanks, but no

nobody maa Had

none la àHad

normal Àadee

north shamàal
    in the north feesh-shamàal

nose anf

not (ba)làa
    not for me, thanks shùkran laa
    not Tuesday balàa youm ath-thulathàa'
    he's not here hùwa moo moujòod
    I'm not Mr Brown, I'm ... àna moo as-sàyid Brown, àna ...
    See NEGATIVES

notebook muzakìrah

nothing laa shay

NOUNS *see* THE

November noofìmbir

now alàan

number (*amount of things*) Àdad رقم
    (*numeral*) ràqam
    what number is it? ay ar-ràqam?

NUMBERS

Although Arabic script is written from right to left,
figures are read as in the West, from left to right. As
you can imagine, when an Arab comes to a number
he has to jump to the beginning of it and read it
'backwards' to the rest of the sentence!

Although the numbers we use in the West are
commonly called Arabic numbers to differentiate
them from Roman numerals, they are still rather
different from 'real' Arabic numerals.

Here are the cardinal numbers:

0	٠	sifr
1	١	wàaHid
2	٢	ithnàyn
3	٣	thalàatha
4	٤	arbà'a
5	٥	khàmsah
6	٦	sìtah
7	٧	sàb'a
8	٨	thamaanèeya
9	٩	tìs'a
10	١٠	Àsharah
11	١١	Hid'àshar
12	١٢	ithn'àshar
13	١٣	thalaath'àshar
14	١٤	arba'at'àshar
15	١٥	khamast'àshar
16	١٦	sit'àshar
17	١٧	saba'at'àshar
18	١٨	thamaant'àshar
19	١٩	tis'at'àshar
20	٢٠	Ashrèen
30	٣٠	thalaathèen
40	٤٠	arba'èen
50	٥٠	khamsèen
60	٦٠	sitèen
70	٧٠	sabAèen
80	٨٠	thamaanèen
90	٩٠	tisAèen
100	١٠٠	mìyah
101	١٠١	mìyah wa wàaHid
200	٢٠٠	miyatàyn

500	٥٠٠	khamsmìyah
1,000	١,٠٠٠	alf
5,000	٥,٠٠٠	khàmsat alàaf
10,000	١٠,٠٠٠	àsharat alàaf
100,000	١٠٠,٠٠٠	mìyat alf
1,000,000	١,٠٠٠,٠٠٠	mileeyòon

The numbers 3–10 precede any noun which is used with them and the noun will naturally go into the plural:

four men
arbà'a rijàal

five invoices
khàmsat fawàatir

All the other numbers also precede the noun which, less obviously – even bewilderingly – stays in the singular. Don't forget the masculine singular indefinite takes **-an** (*see* **a, an**):

thirty-nine men
tìs'a wa thalaathèen ràjulan

sixteen dirhams
sit'àshar dìrhaman

fifty cars
khamsèen sayàarah

To make compound numbers you just put **wa** (and) between the component numbers. However, for numbers between 21 and 99 you invert the order first. So:

103 mìyah wa thalàatha
2,406 alfàyn wa arba'mìyah wa sìtah

But: **56** sìtah wa khamsèen
35 khàmsa wa thalaathèen

And: **646** sìtah mìyah wa sìtah wa arba'èen

To say dates in years you just say the number with **fees-sànah** (in the year) before it:

in 1955 I was a small boy
fees-sànah alf wa tis'amìyah khàmsa wa khamsèen àna kùntu wàladan saghèeran

we incorporated our company in 1978
asàsna shirkàtna fees-sànah alf wa tis'amìyah wa thamàaneeya wa sabʌèen

Ordinal numbers from 1 to 100 are given below. They can be made feminine in the normal way: by

adding **-ah** or **-yah**. 'First' in the feminine is
irregular:

1st	àwal (*fem.* òolah)
2nd	thàanee
3rd	thàalith
4th	ràabiA
5th	khàamis
6th	sàadis
7th	sàabiA
8th	thàamin
9th	tàasiA
10th	Àashir

These ordinals are placed after the noun:

the first	al-àwal
the ninth (one)	at-tàasiA
the fifth car	as-sayàarah al-khàamisah
the third man	ar-ràjul ath-thàalith

O

oasis wàaHah

October octùbar

of min

OF

Arabic uses **min** to say 'of' whether 'of' is used in contexts meaning 'made out of' or 'movement out of'. For example:

a dress of silk
fustàan min al-Harèer

a ring of gold
khàatim min az-zàhab

he came out of the house
hùwa khàraj min al-bàyt

There is another rather ingenious way of expressing such phrases as 'a cup of tea', 'a bed of nails' etc. If the phrase is definite you put the two words (in this case 'cup' and 'tea') next to each other and *omit* the definite article from the first one. If it happens to be feminine change the **-ah** ending to **-at**. For example:

the cup of tea
finjàan shày

the manager of the company
mudèer ash-shìrkah

the name of the hotel
ism al-fùnduq

the bottle of milk
zajàjat Halèeb

If the phrase is indefinite you just put the two words together with no articles at all but still change the ending of any feminine first word from **-ah** to **-at**. For example:

a cup of tea
finjàan shay

a story of money and power
riwàayat filòos wa qùwah

a history of mental illness
taarèekh marD Àqlee

To use 'of' in a possessive sense, to say that, for example, something belongs to somebody, you can use the word **maal**. This means literally 'property of':

David's car
sayàarah maal David

off (*machine etc.*) waaqìfah

offer (*noun*) ArD
we can offer . . . mùmkin nà'araD . . .

office (*workplace*) màktab [(*pl*) makàatib]

official (*noun*) muwàzaf

often ghàaliban

oil zayt
(*petroleum*) nafт

oil well bi'r nafт

O K ookày

old (*person*) Ajòoz
(*thing*) qadèem
how old are you? qad aysh Aùmruk?

old-fashioned Tiràaz qadèem

Oman Aumàan

Omani Aumàanee

on (*upon*) Àla
(*above*) fouq
(*concerning*) An
on the table Àlat-Tàawalah
on Tuesday youm ath-thulathà'a
is it on? (*machine etc.*) hal hìya shaaghìlah?
a book on Egypt kitàab An mìsr

one wàaHid
one person shakhs wàaHid
the first one (*masc.*) al-àwal
(*fem.*) al-òolah
See NUMBERS

only fàqaт

open (*adjective*) maftòoH
are they open tomorrow? hal hum faatiHèen bùkrah?
when do you open? ìmta tìftaH?
can I open the window? mùmkin àftaH ash-shubàak?

operation (*in hospital*) Amalèeyah

operator (*telephone*) (*man*) Àamil
  (*woman*) Aamìlah
  (*the place dialled*) as-sintràal

opinion rà'ee
  in my opinion fee rà'ee

opposite muqàabil

or aw

orange juice Asèer burtuqàal

order (*in business*) Tàlab
  thank you for your order shùkran Àla Talàbak

order number ràqam at-Tàlab

organize: well organized munàʐam
  poorly organized moo munàʐam

other ghayr
  the other one al-àakhar

our
> There are no possessive adjectives as such in Arabic;
> instead a suffix is added to the word. In the case of
> 'our' you add **-na** to a word ending in a consonant
> and **-tna** to a word ending in a vowel or **ah** (in which
> case the **h** is dropped). For example:

> **house**
> bayt

> **our house**
> bàytna

> **company**
> shìrkah

> **our company**
> shirkàtna

> If you use an adjective with 'our' then you must
> make it definite and add **al-** to the adjective:

> **our American company**
> shirkàtna al-amreekèeyah

ours màalna

out (*lights*) màTfee
  she's out (*of house etc.*) hìya moo moujòodah
  it will be out next month (*new model etc.*) sayàkoon
  jaàhiz feesh-shàhar al-jaay

over (*finished*) intàhaa
  over 40 fouq al-arba'èen
  over there hunàak

overcoat baalTòo

overnight (*travel*) Tool al-làyl

oversleep: I'm afraid I overslept àasif ràaHat Alàya
nòomah Tawèelah

owe: we owe you . . . ìHna madeenèen lak . . .
    you owe us . . . ànta madèen làna . . .

own: my own . . . khaas bee . . .
    your own . . . khaas beek . . .

owner màalik

P

packet Àlbah
  a packet of ... Àlbat ...

pain àlam

Palestine filasTèen

Palestinian filasTèenee

paper wàraq [(*pl*) awràaq]
  (*newspaper*) jarèedah [(*pl*) jaràayid]
  a piece of paper qìTAt wàraq

pardon? Àfwan?

parents al-waalidàyn

park (*noun*) Hadèeqah

part (*noun*) juz' [(*pl*) ajzàa']

partner (*in business*) sharèek [(*pl*) shurakàa]

part-payment Arbòon

party (*celebration*) Hàflah

PASSIVE

There is a passive form of most verbs in Arabic, but
it is used almost exclusively in the literary or
classical language. Unless it is being read aloud from
a newspaper or book the passive form is rarely used
in everyday speech, even by highly educated Arabs.

In English you might say: 'the contract was signed
by us in Cairo' or: 'we were invited out to dinner by
the manager'. Arabic says:

> **we signed the contract in Cairo**
> waqàAna Àlal-Àqd feel-qaahìrah

or: **the manager invited us out to dinner**
> al-mudèer da'àna ìlal-Ashàa

passport jawàaz sàfar جواز سفر

past: past the crossroads/hotel ba'ad at-taqaTùA/al-
fùnduq

PAST TENSE

The past tense of a verb is easy to form from the information given for each verb in this book. Take the first form of the verb given, for example:

write kàtab

This form of the verb is always the past tense in the third person singular. So, for example, **kàtab** means 'he wrote' or 'he has written'. Using this form you can make any other forms, as follows (note that the stress is moved):

(àna)	katàbtu	I wrote (add **-tu**)
(ànta)	katàbta	you wrote (*masc.*)(add **-ta**)
(ànti)	katàbti	you wrote (*fem.*)(add **-tee**)
(hùwa)	kàtab	he wrote (this is the form always given)
(hìya)	katàbat	she wrote (add **-at**)
(ìHna)	katàbna	we wrote (add **-na**)
(àntum)	katàbtum	you wrote (*pl*) (add **-tum**)
(hum)	kàtaboo	they wrote (add **-oo**)

This tense serves as the past definite tense: 'I wrote', and also the perfect tense: 'I have written'. Both are the same in Arabic.

Look at the following examples:

rìHtu ìla al-qaahìrah maratàyn

means: I have been to Cairo twice

or: I went to Cairo twice

hal wàsal hàaza as-sabàaH?

means: has he arrived this morning?

or: did he arrive this morning?

àbadan maa shuftùhu

means: I've never seen it

or: I never saw it

Here is another example:

explain shàraH [yàshraH]

(àna)	sharàHtu	I explained
(ànta)	sharàHta	you explained (*masc.*)
(ànti)	sharàHti	you explained (*fem.*)
(hùwa)	shàraH	he explained
(hìya)	sharàHat	she explained
(ìHna)	sharàHna	we explained
(àntum)	sharàHtum	you explained

(hum)   **sharaHòo**   they explained

In the past tense the personal pronouns (I, you etc.) are optional and are mainly used for emphasis, since the person is already made clear by the verb form.

path mamàr

pavement rasèef

pay dàfa' [yàdfa']
   can I pay now please? mùmkin àdfa' alàan?
   I'll pay for this (àna) sa-'àdfa' thàman hàaza
   See GUESTS

payment dùf'ah

pen qàlam

pencil qàlam rusàas

people naas
   a lot of people naas kuthàar

pepper (*spice*) fìlfil

per: per night kul làylah
   per day kul youm

per cent feel-mèeyah
   25 per cent khàmsah wa Ashrèen feel-mèeyah
   a 10 per cent discount takhfèeD Àsharah feel-mèeyah

perfect (*adjective*) kàamil

PERFECT TENSE *see* PAST TENSE

perfume Àtr

perhaps rùbamaa

permit (*noun: entry permit etc.*) tasrèeH

Persian Gulf al-khalèej al-Àrabee

Note that the Arabs call the Persian Gulf the Arabian Gulf.

person shakhs

PERSONAL PRONOUNS
Here is the full table of personal pronouns. Subject pronouns (I, we etc.) stand as words on their own. Object pronouns are suffixes. These suffixes are always unstressed and when they are added to a

word, the stress in that word moves onto the syllable before the suffix.

SUBJECT PRONOUNS

I	àna
you (*masc.*)	ànta
(*fem.*)	ànti
he	hùwa
she	hìya
we	ìнna
you (*pl*)	àntum
they	hum

DIRECT OBJECT PRONOUNS (as in 'he hit *me*')

me	-nee
you (*masc.*)	-ak
(*fem.*)	-akee
him	-hu
her	-ha
us	-na
you (*pl*)	-kum
them	-hum

INDIRECT OBJECT PRONOUNS (as in 'he gave it *to me*')

By way of example, the suffixes have been attached to **l-** (= to) giving the most common meaning of the indirect object 'to me' etc.):

(to) me	lee
(to) you (*masc.*)	(là)ka
(*fem.*)	(là)ki
(to) him	(là)hu
(to) her	(là)ha
(to) us	(là)na
(to) you (*pl*)	(là)kum
(to) them	(là)hum

See also the individual word entries for 'him', 'me', 'you' etc.

The subject pronouns may often be omitted, since the verb forms (past and future) already show the person in them. Look at these examples which show when the pronoun should be used for emphasis:

he signed that contract
wàqa' Àla zàalik al-Àqd

This does not need **hùwa** since **wàqa'** can only mean 'he signed'.

she, not he, signed that contract
hìya, moo hùwa, wàqa'at Àla zàalik al-Àqd

This does need the pronouns to be inserted for clarity. **wàqa'at** can indeed only mean 'she signed' but following **hùwa** would look like an error unless the pronoun for 'she' were used to start the sentence.

Subject pronouns are also often omitted in questions:

> **àmta wasàlta?**
> when did you arrive?

unless you want to emphasize the word 'you':

> **àmta wasàlta ànta?**
> when did *you* arrive?

Note that in such cases the pronoun comes at the end of the question.

In the present tense, since the verb 'to be' (am, is, are etc.) is omitted, the personal pronoun must not be omitted:

> **I was hungry**
> kùntu jou'àan

but: **I am hungry**
> àna jou'àan

petrol banzèen

petrol station muHàTat banzèen

photograph sòorah footooghraafèeyah

picture (*painting, drawing*) sòorah

piece qìTAt
   a piece of . . . qìTAth . . .

pig khanzèer

PIGS

Pigs and pork are forbidden to Muslims by the Koran and, being taboo, are not found anywhere in the Muslim world – nor will you find even imported pork on the menu in restaurants. Even large hotels which cater for non-Arabs are extremely unlikely to serve pork, since it is so hard to get hold of locally. Pigs are considered unclean, even filthy, and like other filthy things should not be talked about in polite company.

pillow wisàadah

pin dabòos

pipe (*to smoke*) pèepah
  (*water-pipe*) nargèelah
  (*for liquid*) maasòorah

pipeline khaт anaabèeb an-nàfт

place (*noun*) makàan

PLACE NAMES
Place names are nearly always feminine, since the words they are normally associated with (**madèenah** for 'city', **qàryah** for 'village') are feminine.

> **Bagdhad is very hot in summer**
> baghdàd hàrah jìdan fees-sàyf

> **we stayed in beautiful Damascus**
> baqàyna fee-dimàshq al-jamèelah

plastic blaastèek

plate тàbaq

platform rasèef رصيف
  which platform? ay rasèef?
  is this the platform for . . .? hal hàaza ar-rasèef ìla . . .?

pleasant laтèef

please: yes please àiwa, lou samàнt
  can you please . . .? mùmkin . . . lou samàнt?
  please do tafàдal

plenty kathèer
  plenty of . . . kathèer min . . .

PLURALS
There are two sorts of plural in Arabic: regular and irregular. The irregularity lies in the word to be made plural. In this book, when we have just given one word for a noun, e.g. **muwàzaf** (an official) or **sayàarah** (a car), it means that the noun forms a regular plural according to the simple rules below.

To make a regular *masculine* plural you simply add **-òon** to the singular. So for example:

  muwàzaf (official)

becomes: **muwazafòon** (officials)

or: **al-muwazafòon** (the officials)

  muнàasib (an accountant)

becomes: **muнaasibòon** (accountants)

or: **al-muнaasibòon** (the accountants)

To make a regular *feminine* plural you remove the -ah ending and substitute -àat. So for example:

sayàarah (a car)

becomes: **sayaaràat** (cars)

or: **as-sayaaràat** (the cars)

muzàkirah (a notebook)

becomes: **muzakiràat** (notebooks)

or: **al-muzakiràat** (the notebooks)

It will be noticed that these regular plural endings always bear the stress.

When a noun is irregular – and there are a lot of them – we have given the plural form in square brackets where relevant.

You will notice that the irregular plurals shown in the book do not have special endings. This is because the plurals are made in a complicated way by altering the internal 'shape' of the word, not by adding prefixes or suffixes. In fact there is no way of guessing what an irregular plural may be and they must simply be learnt along with the singular.

pocket jayb

point: please point to it shàawir Alàyha lou samàHt
  that's a good point haàzee nùqTah jàyidah
  two point five ithnàyn wa khàmsah min Àsharah
  (*literally: two plus five tenths*)

police boolèes بوليس

policeman shùrTee

polite moo'àdab
  See MANNERS

politics siyàasah

POLYGAMY *see* MARRIAGE

pork laHm khanzèer
  See PIGS

port (*for ships*) meenàa

porter (*in hotel: for bags*) bawàab

POSSESSIVE ADJECTIVES

There are no possessive adjectives as such in Arabic.
Instead a suffix is added to the word.

Here are the full forms. The **t** is inserted at the end of a feminine word ending in **-ah**. Here they are added to our old friend **kitàab** – a book:

my book	-(t)ee	kitàabee
your book		
(*masc.*)	-(t)ak	kitàabak
(*fem.*)	-(t)ik	kitàabik
his book	-(t)hu	kitàabhu
her book	-(t)ha	kitàabha
our book	-(t)na	kitàabna
your book (*pl*)	-(t)kum	kitàabkum
their book	-(t)hum	kitàabhum

Of course these suffixes can be added to plural nouns as well.

If you are using an adjective with one of these possessive pronouns then you must add **al-** to the adjective. For example:

> **my new shirt**
> qamèesee al-jadèed

> **your Arabic dictionary**
> qaamòosak al-Àrabee

Let us look at some of these possessive adjectives in action:

> **he gave me his newspaper**
> hùwa ÀTaa lee jarèedat-hu

> **I ate my dinner alone**
> akàltu Ashàa'ee li-wàHdee

> **we left our suitcases in our hotel**
> taràkna shunùTna fee-fundùqna

> **where is your ticket, Madam?**
> wayn tazkàrtik, ya sayìdah?

> **the army will protect our country**
> al-jàysh sa-yuHàafiz Àla balàdna

possible mùmkin
  is it possible to . . .? mùmkin . . .?

post (*verb*) àrsal bel-barèed

post office màktab barèed مكتب بريد

postcard kaart

potatoes baтàaтis

pound (*weight*) raтl, paòond
(*sterling*) jinàyah istirlèenee

prayer-mat misàllah

prefer: which do you prefer? ay wàaнidah tufàdil?
I prefer ... (àna) ufàdil ...

PREPOSITIONS

There are twelve common prepositions in Arabic.
Here they are:

in	fee
at/in	bi
to/for	li
from	min
on	àla
with (*'chez'*)	And
under	taнt
above	fouq
after	bà'ad
before	qabl
with (*next to*)	ma'
to (*movement*)	ìla

The preposition always comes immediately before
the word it relates to. If this word is definite the
preposition is merged with the **al-**. Let us look at
some in action:

I remained in the hotel (fee = **in**)
baqàytu feel-fùnduq

I left my shoes under the bed (taнt = **under**)
taràktu aнzèeyatee taнt as-sarèer

the inspector gave me my passport (li = **to**/lee
= **to me**)
al-mufàtish Aтàa lee jawàazee

I took the suitcase from the car (min = **from**)
akhàztu ash-shànтah min as-sayàarah

put the money on the table! (ala = **on**)
da' al-filòos àlaт-тàawalah!

the director was with the minister (ma' = **with**)
al-mudèer kaan ma' al-wazèer

present (*gift*) hadèeyah

PRESENT TENSE

There is no present tense of the verb 'to be' in
Arabic. In order to say something/somebody *is*

something you merely put the personal pronoun, **hùwa** or **hìya** depending on the gender of the subject, before the adjective without using a verb at all. Of course the adjective must be made plural or feminine or both as appropriate. For example:

> **I am tired** (*masc.*)
> àna ta'abàan
> (*literally: I tired*)

> **I am tired** (*fem.*)
> àna ta'abàanah

> **we are hungry**
> ìHna jou'anèen
> (*literally: we hungry*)

> **I am from London**
> àna min londòn

In all cases where English uses a present tense of a verb, Arabic just uses the future (the tense given in square brackets in this book) either with no prefix at all or with the prefix **ba-** if the action is still continuing. For example:

> **I am waiting for my friend**
> àna ba-antàzir sadèeqee

> **she is going to the meeting**
> hìya ba-taròoH ìlal-ijtimàa'

> **are you writing a letter?**
> hal ba-tàktub risàalah?

> **where do you live?**
> wayn tàskun?

> **what are you doing there?**
> shoo ba-tusàawee hunàak?

> **I am feeling ill**
> àna ba-àshAor bi-màraD

president (*of state*) ra'èes

pretty (*of women*) jamèelah
  (*of things*) raqèeq

price sìAr
  that's our best price hàaza àHsan sìAr làna

prince amèer

princess amèerah

private khaaS
  in private (*talk etc.*) Àla infiràad

probably yùmkin

problem mushkìlah [(*pl*) mashàakil]
 we've had some problems kaan Andàna bà'aD al-
 mashàakil
 that's no problem! moo mushkìlah!

product mùntaj [(*pl*) muntajàat]

production manager mudèer al-intàaj

profit ribH

pronounce nàTaq [yànTuq]
 how is it pronounced? kayf tanTùqha?

PRONOUNS *see* PERSONAL PRONOUNS

PRONUNCIATION
The transliteration of Arabic words given in this
book is designed for the reader whoses native
language is English. Read the words out loud to
yourself at all times to get the 'feel' of the sounds of
Arabic and put extra emphasis on those syllables
with an accent over them.

 Do make sure you give extra weight to the
emphatic letters which are transliterated by small
capital letters in the text. This does not mean
spitting them out. But pronounce them almost as
though they were a double letter. If you say 'bad
doctor' you have just pronounced the emphatic D.
Similarly 'fast train' gives you T and 'jazz zombie' z.
The letter A (which is usually merely marked by an
apostrophe when it is already next to an 'a') should
be pronounced as a heavy 'a' sound just as you might
exclaim at the zoo in an astonished voice: 'that's an
anteater!'

 Don't try to say the words too quickly and make
sure you pronounce every syllable! English speakers
have a tendency to swallow their sounds and so
special care should be taken to give every vowel in
Arabic time to be heard. The Arabic you will hear
will vary enormously depending where you are –
each region has its own special sort of intonation –
but, wherever you are, you will find that educated
Arabs will be able to answer you in the language of
this book. If you stick to the pronunciation given
here *you* will certainly be understood wherever you
go in the Arab world.

publicity di'Aayah

pull sàHab [yàs-Hub]   اسحب

pure (*substance*) naqèe

push dàfa' [yàdfuA]   ادفع

pyramid al-hàram [(*pl*) al-ahràam]

Q

Qatar qàTar

quality nouAèeyah
   quality goods biDàa'iA zaat nouAèeyah mumtàazah

quality control muràaqabat an-nouAèeyah

quarter rùbA

queen màlikah

QUESTIONS
Arabic makes a question from a statement very simply. You put the word **hal** at the beginning of the statement, leaving the word order the same. You also change the intonation of the sentence, the voice usually rising noticeably at the end. For example:

> **the manager is here**
> al-mudèer hùna

> **is the manager here?**
> hal al-mudèer hùna?

> **he is the man responsible**
> hùwa ar-ràjul al-mas'òol

> **is he the man responsible?**
> hal hùwa ar-ràjul al-mas'òol?

In very colloquial usage you do not even have to put **hal** at the beginning – you just put the statement in a querying tone of voice.

Of course you can also use specific interrogative words to ask a specific question. Here are the most common:

what?	ay?
why?	laysh?
where?	wayn?
from where?	minèen?
when?	èmta?
which?	ay?
how much?	kam?
how?	kayf?
how many?	adày?
who?	meen?

These interrogative words open the sentence.

what day is today?
ay youm al-yòum?

how do you do this?
kayf tusàawee hàaza?

which one do you want?
ay wàaHid turèed?

how are you?
kayf Hàalak?

how many share-holders are there in this company?
kam Adàd al-musàahimoon fee hazìhi ash-shìrkah?

In colloquial use you will often hear these interrogative words tacked on to the end of a sentence rather than at the beginning.

When you are framing a question you can often make use of the very useful word **mùmkin?**, which means literally 'is it possible?'. If you use it without a question mark it means 'it is possible'. So if you want to say:

can I see the newspaper, please?

you can say:

mùmkin ashòof al-jarèedah lou samàHt?

which means literally:

is it possible I will see the newspaper, please?

and the reply to this might be:

mùmkin
yes
(*literally: it is possible*)

quick sarèeA

quickly bi-sùr'ah
   as quickly as possible bi-àsra' maa yùmkin

quiet hàadee

quite . . . bà'aD ash-shày
   Note that the Arabic word for 'quite' comes after the word it refers to, so instead of saying 'quite hot' Arabic says literally 'hot quite'.

quote (*noun: for job, a price etc.*) taqdèem sìAran

R

radio ràadioo

rail: by rail bil-qiTàar

railway station محطة السكة الحديد
   muHàTat al-qiTàar

rain (*noun*) màTar
   it's raining (ad-dùniya) bi-timaTàr
   (*literally: the world is in rain*)

raincoat baalTòo màTar

RAMADAN
   Ramadan is the ninth month of the Muslim (lunar)
   year and falls at an ever earlier date each year
   according to the Western (solar) calendar. It falls
   eleven days earlier each (non-leap-) year and twelve
   days earlier in a leap year. So whereas Ramadan
   began on 19 April 1988, which coincided with late
   April and early May, in 1989 it began on 8 April, and
   in 1990 it will begin on 29 March.
   Ramadan is a time for abstinence and most
   Muslims will fast from sunrise to sunset, and not
   smoke or drink alcohol at any time. Obviously it is
   more stressful to do this when Ramadan falls in high
   summer when the days are long and hot. The
   restrictions do not apply to anybody who is ill or
   feeding children or travelling around the country.
   Westerners do not have to fast but you will find that
   almost all restaurants will be closed during the day
   and it is a notoriously bad time to do business.
   Business travellers are strongly advised against trying
   to do business during Ramadan unless they are
   specifically invited during that period.

rate of exchange sÌAr at-taHwèel سعر التحويل

razor maakìnat Hilàaqah

read qàra' [yàqra']
   could you read it out for me? mùmkin taqrà'ha lee?

ready (*goods*) jàahiz
   (*person*) musta'èd

real (*leather etc.*) Haqèeqee

receipt eesàal
    can I have a receipt? mùmkin eesàal lou samàHt?

receive (*goods etc.*) istàlam [yastàlim]

reception (*of hotel*) istiqbàal

red àHmar

Red Sea al-bàHr al-àHmar

reduced price sìAr mukhàfaD

reference number ràqam al-ishàarah

refinery mà'mal takrèer

registered mail barèed musàjal

reliable (*person, company, machine*) yùmkin al-iAtimàad
  Alàyhu

remember tazàkar [yatazàkar]
    I remember atazàkar

rent istà'jar [yastà'jir]

repair sàlaH [yusàaliH]
    it needs repairing muHtàajah taslèeH

repeat a'àd [yuA-ìd]
    please repeat that lou samàHt A-ìd zàalik màrah
  thaanèeyah

reply (*written*) jawàab
  (*spoken*) ijàabah
    we look forward to your reply nà'mal an yasìlna
  jawàabak

REPLYING
Some useful replies you may want to give are:

    don't mention it
    laa shùkr Alal-wàajib

    sorry
    Àfwan

    I'm fine
    àna bi-khàyr

    you're welcome!
    tafàDal!

representative (*noun: of company*) mumàthil

reserve (*seat*) Hàjaz [yàHjiz]
    can I reserve a seat? mùmkin àHjiz kursèe?

restaurant màTAm مطعم

RESTAURANTS

Restaurants are set out just as they are in the West, except that you will find many more patios and outdoor seating areas than in damp Northern Europe.

In the residential areas of cities you will see a cheaper sort of restaurant, used mainly by local people, where there is only one dish on the menu. You go in, pick up a dish and move along the counter getting a helping of today's special. You pick up your fork and napkin and sit on a stool facing what is usually a long counter stretching right around the room. These are restaurants for the hungry and not for the diner with time to spare or a particularly sensitive palate. And they are strictly male preserves.

return: a return ticket to . . . tàzkarah Aòudah li . . .

rice arùz

rich (*person*) ghanèe

right (*correct*) SaHèeH
(*direction*) yamèen
that's right hàaza SaHèeH
all right (*I agree*) wahùwa ka-zàalik
I'm all right, thanks (*not hurt etc.*) àna bi-khàyr shùkran
that's all right (*doesn't matter*) walà Alàyk
on the right Alal-yamèen

rights (*to manufacture etc.*) Huqòoq

river nahr

road shàariA
(*way*) Tarèeq
is this the road to Damascus? hal hàaza at-Tarèeq ìla dimàshq?

room ghùrfah [(*pl*) ghùruf] غرفة
I'd like a room for two nights 'urèed ghùrfah li-mùdat laylatàyn
in my room fee ghurfàtee

rubber (*material*) kaawìtsh
(*eraser*) goòmah

rubbish (*waste*) zibàalah
(*poor-quality goods*) biDàa'iA ta'abàanah

rude qabèeH

RUDENESS
One point worth mentioning here – apart from the obvious advice to behave at least as politely as you would at home – is to remember that it is considered positively rude not to offer someone at least a bite of whatever you are eating when they meet you. The offer will never be accepted, but must be made all the same. *See* MANNERS, MISTAKES.

S

sad (*person, news*) наzèen

safe (*not dangerous*) amàan
(*not in danger*) ma'amòon

salad salàтah

salary ràatib [(*pl*) rawàatib]

sale: for sale lil-bàyа

sales director mudèer al-mabee'àat

salesman bàa'eeа

salt milн

same nafs al-. . .
the same aircraft nafs ат-тaa'ìrah
the same again please *no equivalent in Arabic; you
need to mention the noun and say, for example:*

sàandwich thàanee lou samàнt
another sandwich please

sample (*noun: of goods, of work*) ау-ìnah

sandwich sàandwich

Saturday youm as-sàbt

Saudi (*adjective, noun*) sa'òodee

Saudi Arabia as-sa'oodèeyah

say qaal [yaqòol]
what did he say? aysh qaal?
he said . . . qaal . . .
how do you say . . . in Arabic? kayf taqòol . . . bil-
Àrabee?
how do you say it? (*pronounce*) kayf taqòolha?

scarf koofèeyah

schedule jàdwal [(*pl*) jadàawil]
work is on schedule ash-shùghl màashee наsab al-
muнàdad
work is behind schedule ash-shùghl muta'àkhar

school madràsah [(*pl*) madàaris]

scissors maqàs

Scotland iskotlànda

sea baHr
  by sea (*travel, send*) bil-bàHr

seat màq'ad [(*pl*) maqàa'id]

second (*adjective*) ath-thàanee
  See **date**

second class (*travel*) dàrajah thaanèeyah

second-hand mustà'amal

secretary (*male*) sikritèer
  (*female*) sikritèerah
  my secretary (*male*) sikritèeree
  (*female*) sikritèeratee
  his secretary sikriteeràt-hu

see shaaf [yashòof]
  can I see it? mùmkin ashòofha?
  have you seen my colleague? hal shùfta zamèelee?
  I saw him a few minutes ago shuftùhu min daqeeqatàyn fàatoo
  let's wait and see khalìna nantàzar wa nashòof
  oh, I see ah, fahìmtuk

sell bàA' [yabèeA]
  we sell . . . nabèeA . . .

send àrsal [yùrsil]
  we'll send it out to you nursìlha lak

September siptìmbir

serious (*situation*) khaTèer
  this is very serious hàaza amr khaTèer jìdan

sex jins

SEX

  Arab attitudes to sex are, by Western standards, very
  conservative and non-permissive and it is fair to compare them to those attitudes held by the Victorian British – no sex before marriage, complete
  and lasting fidelity to your spouse, lots of children,
  no contraception and absolutely no homosexuality
  or any variations on that theme.
  Most Westerners can cope with a certain amount
  of conversation about sexual matters, problems or
  exploits, depending on the occasion, without writh-
  ing in embarrassment; but you will find that mention of *anything* with a sexual overtone will cause an
  Arab colleague to be plunged into confusion and

awkwardness. Arab attitudes to sex are conditioned by traditional values and they are maintained by the social separation of the sexes practised to varying degrees in all Arab countries. This means that most Arabs see marriage as the only way of having a relationship with a woman at all, and vice-versa of course, and it is this that accounts for the fact that almost all Arabs do get married and spend their life up to that point in curious anticipation.

You will not find pornography anywhere in the Arab world, and indeed it is rare to see a man and woman holding hands let alone kissing in public.

In the light of this, it will be understood how any kind of remotely flirtatious let alone salacious behaviour by a Westerner is regarded as beyond the pale in any Arab country. And in the more traditional countries – such as Saudi Arabia – anything offending against the Arab views of sexual propriety can lead to very serious trouble.

The best advice a Western traveller can take with him to the Arab world regarding sex is: forget it – unless you are taking your husband or wife with you!

shake haz [yàhaz]

shaking hands salàam bil-yàᴅ

SHAKING HANDS

Shaking hands is the universal greeting in the Arab world and you should shake hands with everyone you meet. You should be ready to shake hands with everyone in a room when you arrive somewhere; your host will introduce you and you should take your cue from him.

Once you know someone well, perhaps after you have met four or five times, you will shake hands and also exchange a kiss on each cheek at the same time. This only applies between men. Men should never kiss women at any time however well they know them.

shame: that's a shame àasif

SHAME

Arab society is not a 'shame society' in the sense that, for example, Japan is, where the potential stigma of losing face is a constant spur to greater effort and achievement. Arab society is not particu-larly achievement-oriented and takes a fairly relaxed view of competition in the Western social and business senses.

Arab society's sense of shame focuses rather on family honour, or the lack of it, especially as regards its unmarried womenfolk. In this regard it is more similar to Sicilian or Iberian society. Shame is avoided if family integrity is upheld – this is a pressure which constantly exerts itself on members of a family and it both reinforces non-permissive behaviour and encourages a moral obligation to provide for less fortunate members of the family.

shampoo (*noun*) shaambòo

sharp (*blade*) Haad
(*taste*) Hàariq

shave (*verb*) Hàlaq [yàHliq]

shaver maakèenat Hilàaqah

shaving soap Saabòon Hilàaqah

she hìya

Note that the verb 'to be' is usually implied (in the present tense). If you want to say 'she is' you just say '**hìya . . .**'. For example:

she is my mother
hìya ùmmee
(*literally: she my mother*)

she is very tired
hìya ta'abàanah jìdan
(*literally: she very tired*)

she is a teacher at the college of medicine
hìya mudarìsah fee kulèeyat aт-тìb

The pronoun **hìya** can be omitted if it is clear from the context that 'she' is the intended subject of a verb:

she arrived yesterday
(hìya) wasàlt ams

I don't know her but she will be waiting for me at the airport
maa bi-aarìfha walàkin (hìya) sa-tantazìrnee feel-maтàar

sheikh shaykh

ship safèenah [(*pl*) sùfun]
  by ship bis-safèenah

shipping company (*for freight*) shìrkat shaHn

shirt qamèes [(*pl*) qumsàan]

shoe Hizàa [(*pl*) aHzèeyah]

shop (*noun*) dukàan [(*pl*) dakaakèen]

short (*person, time*) qasèer

shoulder kàtif

show: can you show me? mùmkin tarawèenee?
can you show me how it works? mùmkin tishràH lee
kayf tà'amal?

shower doosh (*borrowed from the French* douche)
I'd like to take a shower urèed àakhuz doosh

shut (*verb*) qàfal [yàqfil]
it's shut hùwa maqfòol

sick (*ill*) marèeD
I'm feeling sick (*like vomiting*) àshAor bi-taqayàa

side (*of box etc.*) jàanib [(*pl*) jawàanib]

sights manàazir
the sights of . . . al-manàaTiq ash-shahèerah fee . . .
(*literally: the famous areas in . . .*)

sign (*verb: document*) wàqa'a [yuwàqiA]
please sign here wàqiA hùna lou samàHt
where do I sign? wayn uwàqiA?

signature touqèeA

silver fìDah

similar mushàabih
it's similar but not the same hìya mushaabìhah
walakìnha làysat nafsàha tamàaman

since: since our last meeting mùnzu muqaabalàtna al-
akhèerah
since last year mùnzu as-sànah al-maaDèeyah

sing ghàna [yughànee]

single: I'm single (*man*) àna àa'zab
(*woman*) àna azbàa

single room ghùrfah li-shàkhs wàaHid

single ticket tazkàrah zihàab fàqaT

sir as-sàyid
See ADDRESSING PEOPLE

sister ukht [(*pl*) akhawàat]

sit jàlas [yàjlis]
can I sit here? mùmkin àjlis hùna?
please sit down tafàDal!

SITTING DOWN
The most important person in a meeting or at a meal, perhaps the chairman or host, always sits at the head of the table and the second most important person sits opposite him. The next most important group of people sits on the right of the chairman while the least important people sit on his left.

In Saudi Arabia and the other Gulf States, where they may use low tables or trays for food, these are lined up beside each other and the senior member of the tribe or host sits at the head of the first one with the rest of the guests following the same arrangement as above.

size (*of clothing*) Hajm [(*pl*) Hujòom]

skin jild

skirt tanòorah

SKIRTS
The very great majority of Arab women wear skirts or dresses – often full-length in the more traditional societies. You may see a woman in jeans or a trouser-suit in the large cities but it is comparatively rare in the Arab world as a whole.

sky samàa

sleep (*verb*) naam [yanàam]
I need some sleep urèed anàam shwàyah
did you sleep well? nìmta kooàyis?

slow baTèe'
very slowly baTèe' jìdan

small saghèer

smell (*noun*) raa'ìHah

smile (*noun*) ibtisàamah

SMILING
The only point to remember here – apart from smiling as you would normally in the West – is not to smile at women you do not know very well. By

smiling at them you will embarrass not only them but also any men that happen to be with them.

smoke dukhàan
  do you smoke? (*offering cigarette*) hal tudàkhin?
  (*verb*) dàkhan [yudàkhin]
  may I smoke? mùmkin udàkhin?

SMOKING

Smoking is as common in the Arab world today as it was in the West fifteen years ago and so far there is little concern about the health aspects of smoking which have made such an impact on smoking habits in the West. Smoking is not tolerated in or around mosques and holy sites and people do not smoke during the fast of Ramadan (*see* RAMADAN).

snow (*noun*) thalj

so (*very*) jìdan
  it's so warm al-jòu dàafee jìdan
  not so fast moosh bi-sùr'ah jìdan

soap Saabòon (*borrowed from the French* savon)

sock juràab [(*pl*) juraabàat]

soft drink muraTabàat

software bayaanàat al-komputòr

sole rights Huqòoq munfàridah

some bà'aD

SOME

To say 'some of' you use **bà'aD** with a definite noun. For example:

  bà'aD al-jìbnah
  some of the cheese

  bà'aD as-sayaaràat
  some of the cars

If the noun is qualified by a possessive suffix such as **na** (our) it is automatically definite. For example:

  bà'aD muntajàatna
  some of our products

In many cases, however, the word 'some' is not translated. If you just want to say 'some cheese' you just use the noun in its basic form without **al**. For example:

> **aaTèenee jìbnah lou samàHt**
> give me some cheese please

> **shùftu sayaaràat amàam al-màbna**
> I saw some cars in front of the building

somebody shakhs ma

something shay ma

sometimes aHyàanan

somewhere fee makàan ma

son ibn [(pl) abnàa]

soon qarèeban
> **as soon as possible** fee àqrab fùrsah
> **we'll be back soon** sanàrja' fee àqrab fùrsah

sorry muta'àsif
> **I'm very sorry** àna muta'àsif jìdan

SORRY

The British are renowned for saying 'sorry' even when there is little to feel sorry about and what they really mean is 'excuse me'.

àasif means 'sorry' and you say it when there is something to regret; perhaps you have trodden on somebody's foot or walked right into them. If you just accidentally bump into somebody with no pain registered you just say:

> **Àfwan**
> excuse me

If you hear that somebody is ill or upset you always use **àasif** and say:

> **I'm sorry**
> àna àasif (*said by a man*)

or: àna aasìfah (*said by a woman*)

sort (*type*) noùA [(pl) anwàa']
> **a different sort of** ... noùA àakhar min ...

soup shòorbah

south janòob
> **in the south** feel-janòob

souvenir tizkàar
> **as a souvenir** ka-tizkàar

speak takàlam [yatakàlam]
  do you speak English? hal tatakàlam inglèezee?
  may I speak English? mùmkin atakàlam inglèezee?
  I don't speak . . . maa atakàlam . . .
  can I speak to . . .? (*on telephone*) mùmkin atàsil bi
  . . .?
  I wish I could speak Arabic atamàna atakàlam
  Àrabee
  See PRONUNCIATION

special makhsòos

speed (*noun*) sùr'ah
  we'll try to speed things up sa-nuHàawil injàaz al-
  mashròoA bi-sùr'ah

sphinx àbool-hool

spoon mal'àqah

spring (*season*) ar-rabèeA
  in the spring feer-rabèeA

stairs salàalim

stamp tàabiA
  two stamps for Great Britain, please taabi'àyn li-
  ingiltìra lou samàHt

stand (*noun: at trade fair etc.*) maqàr
  at our stand And maqàrna
  at your stand And maqàrkum

start (*verb*) bàda' [yàbda']
  starting from next month ibtidàa'an min ash-shàhr
  al-qàadim

station maHàTah محطة

stay: I'm staying at . . . àna nàazil fee . . .

steal sàraq [yàsriq]
  my suitcase has been stolen shanTàtee insàraqat

STEALING

There is petty theft in the Arab world just as there is
the world over and travellers should always be on
their guard, especially at airports and hotels. Nevertheless stealing is less prevalent in the Arab world
than in the West and crimes such as house-breaking,
robbery or assault are very rare indeed compared to
the West. When they do occur it is mainly in the
poor areas of larger cities.

  The community spirit of Arab residential neigh-
bourhoods, even in large cities, ensures that crimi-

nals have a hard time getting away with their
felonious little plans, since an unofficial 'neighbourhood watch' system is operated by the residents.
Strangers to the area are likely to be noticed
immediately.

According to a strict interpretation of Islamic law
a thief may lose one of his/her hands after conviction for a second offence and in some countries this
is actually done *pour encourager les autres*. Whenever
it does happen it attracts a lot of Western media
attention – but in fact this sort of irreversible
punishment is very rare.

sterling (*currency*) isterlèenee

sticking plaster shareeт blàastar

still maa zaal
   it's still not right maa zàalat ghayr saнèeнah

stomach baтn

stomach-ache màghas

stop (*verb*) tawàqaf [yatawàqaf]
   (*road sign*) qis قف
   could you stop here please? (*to taxi driver etc.*)
   mùmkin tàqif hùna lou samàнt?
   does this train stop at . . .? hal al-qiтàar yaqif fee . . .?

straight mustaqèem
   straight on dùghree

strange gharèeb

stranger (*foreigner*) ajnàbee
   (*newcomer*) gharèeb
   I'm a stranger to this town àna gharèeb An hàazeel-
   bàlad

street shàariA [(*pl*) shawàariA]
   the next street on the left ash-shàariA al-jàay Àlal-
   yasàar
   what street is it on? hùwa fee ày shàariA?
   could you write the street name down? mùmkin
   tàktub ism ash-shàariA lou samàнt?

strike (*noun*) iɒràab

string doobàarah

strong (*material*) matèen
   (*taste, drink*) qàwee

student тàalib [(*pl*) тulàab]

stupid ghàbee

successful nàajiH
   here's to a successful relationship! ìla Alaàqat Àmal naajìHah!

Sudan as-soodàan

Sudanese (*adjective, noun*) soodàanee

suddenly fajàa'ah

Suez Canal qanàat as-sooèes

sugar sùkar سكر

suit (*noun: clothing*) bàdlah

suitcase shànTah [(*pl*) shùnuT]

summer sayf
   in the summer fees-sàyf

sun shams

sun glasses naZàarat ash-shàms

sunburn làfHat ash-shàms

Sunday youm al-àHad

suntan lotion maHlòol Hamàam ash-shàms

supper Ashàa'

SUPPER *see* DINNER

supplier al-muwàrid

supply (*verb*) wàrad [yuwàrid]

sure: I'm sure (*said by man*) àna muta'àkid
   (*said by woman*) àna muta'àkidah
   I'm not sure àna moosh muta'àkid(ah)
   are you sure? hal ànta muta'àkid(ah)

surname ism al-Aa'ìlah

SURNAMES

The surname or family name of an Arab is normally only used in official documents or to distingish several people with the same first name from each other. It is often prefixed by **al-**. You do not use a person's surname when you are talking to them; Arabs get straight onto first-name terms from the very first meeting, a habit which is not considered over-familiar as it might be in the West. It is interesting to note that, in the Arab world, a woman's name does not change when she gets married.

There is just as great a diversity of Arab surnames as there is of Western ones. You will often find that they derive from the name of the place from which the family originates. For example, a family from the Iraqi capital might be called **al-Baghdadi** or a family from Aleppo in Northern Syria might be called **al-Halabi** (the Arabic for Aleppo being Halab).

swearword kàlimat sibàab

SWEARWORDS

Swearwords are much less common in Arabic than they are in English. This is basically because Arabs respect their language and try to keep swearwords out of it.

Consequently, among educated Arabs at least, you will not hear swearwords interjected into their speech and they will certainly not expect to hear any foul language coming from their foreign visitors, however appropriate the occasion. In the author's experience, any attempt to drop real swearwords casually into the conversation in a bid to sound macho brings a hot flush to the cheeks of the most hardened Arab man-of-the-world, followed immediately by persistent and agitated speculation about where such words could have been learnt.

In view of this we shall restrict ourselves to a few relatively inoffensive *interjections* which can be used sparingly at the right time.

The equivalent of 'Good Lord!' used when the full, awful consequences of something are realized is:

ya sàatir

To express amazement at something good you may safely say:

ya àllah
Oh Allah

in a respectful tone of voice. This is also a good standby for pleasantly surprising moments of most kinds.

Considering the gung-ho approach to driving in many Arab cities you will need something to shout at cars heading for you on the pavement:

Himàar!
ass!

is the best here, or even:

ghàbee!
stupid!

if you are out of reach of the driver's fist.

swim sàbaн [yàsbaн]

swimming pool Hamàam sibàaHah

switch (*noun: light switch, on machine etc.*) miftàaн [(*pl*) mafaatèeн]

Syria soorèeya

Syrian (*adjective, noun*) sòoree

T

table Tàawalah

TABLES
Almost every home in the Arab world from Morocco
to the Gulf has a dining-room with tables and chairs
in the Western style, although this is still very new in
Saudi Arabia and the other Gulf States. (The big
difference from the West is that this dining-room is
normally used only for special occasions or when
guests are present – this would certainly include any
Western visitors – and it is kept clean and tidy for
this purpose. A parallel can be drawn with the 'front
room' similarly kept only for visitors in many British
homes until fairly recently.) For everyday use Arabs
will either eat off a functional table in the living-
room or, especially in the Gulf States and North
African countries, will take their food off a huge tray
which is put on the floor and which acts as a table.
Diners sit around this tray just as if it were a table
(*see* EATING HABITS). In smaller villages and rural
areas, particularly in Egypt, meals are served on a
big wooden tray which sits on four small legs and
becomes a very low table, although if visitors arrive
this arrangement will be abandoned in favour of the
dining-room mentioned above.

take àakhaz [yàakhuz]
I'll take it (*buy*) sa-aakhùz-ha
how long does it take? (*journey*, *job*) adàysh
tastàghriq?

talk takàlam [yatakàlam]
can I talk to . . .? mùmkin atakàlam ma' . . .?

tall Tawèel

tap sanbòr [(*pl*) sanàabir]

tape (*for tape-recorder*) sharèeт tasjèel [(*pl*) sharàa'iт
tasjèel]

tape-recorder musàjil

taxi taaksèe   تاكسى

TAXIS

Taxis throughout the Arab world used to charge a
fare by the meter, but the trend nowadays is to
charge by the distance covered. As you can imagine
the charge rises according to the sharpness of the
driver and the naïveté of the passenger. The best
course of action is to make a point of always asking
for a rough quote before you get in.

You will find that each city has taxis of a different
colour. In Cairo, for example, they are black and
white while in Alexandria they are yellow and black.
Generally speaking there are three types of taxi.
Firstly there is the sort you hail in the street. These
operate only within the city and its environs. Secondly there are taxis, often Mercedes, which ply
between cities and the countryside in between.
These are usually to be found in ranks near the main
bus stations. The third type is what we think of as a
minicab – you telephone a taxi office and they send
out a taxi to pick you up. This is the most
satisfactory service, but it costs rather more than the
taxi you hail in the street.

These days most taxis are air-conditioned, especially those plying between cities, since after an hour
in a sealed sardine-tin under the desert sun most
people would feel unfit for anything at their destina-
tion except the casualty department at the hospital.
You will find that taxi-drivers like to make their cabs
– which are always privately owned – as much like a
home-from-home as possible and to this end they
decorate them with all sorts of personal mementoes
such as photographs of their family, postcards from
friends and usually the pennant of their favourite
football team! You can make a taxi-driver happy by
admiring their collection effusively during the journey.

Here are some useful phrases if you are travelling
by taxi:

how much is it to . . .?
kam tà'akhuz li . . .?

please call me a taxi
lou samàHt naadèe lee taaksèe

can you send a taxi to . . .?
mùmkin tùrsil taaksèe ìla . . .?

please go to this address
lou samàHt wasàlnee li hàaza al-ʌunwàan

please go to Hotel . . .
lou samàHt wasàlnee li-fùnduq . . .

please turn right
lou samàHt lif Àla al-yamèen

please turn left
lou samàHt lif Àla alyasàar

please go straight on
lou samàHt Àla Tool

please stop here
lou samàHt òuqaf hùna

tea shaay شاى

a cup of tea finjàan shaay

TEA

Arabs consume vast quantities of tea, but the concept of tea-time is unknown in the Arab world: any time is tea-time. In the Gulf States and in the villages and rural areas tea is drunk very strong and already sweetened, being served in small china cups which are held between the thumb and forefinger of the right hand. It is usually boiled over a fire or stove for some fifteen minutes before being served, and at least three or four cups are drunk at a time.

In the big cities and hotels tea is drunk in ordinary cups with sugar added according to individual taste. Arabs normally drink tea out of a glass, but when they have visitors – such as a Westerner – they use conventional cups.

Tea-drinking is something of a ritual in the Arab world and you will always be offered a cup when you visit anywhere – even a shop sometimes – and it should always be accepted gracefully. It will usually have been made with a lot of sugar and it would be a serious faux-pas to refuse or even demur at the offered hospitality just on account of its sweetness.

teacher mudàris

telegram barqèeyah

telephone (*noun*) tilifòon
(*verb*) tàlfan [yutàlfin]
can I use your telephone? mùmkin astà'amil tilifòonak?

telephone directory dalèel at-tilifòon

TELEPHONING

Here are some phrases to help you when confronted by a ringing telephone or having to make a call to an Arab household/office, etc.:

A: **hello, I would like to speak to Mr David Harvey**
aalòo, urèed an ataнàdath ìla as-sàyid David Harvey

hello, I would like to speak to Mrs Janet Kelly
aalòo, urèed an ataнàdath ìla as-sàyidah Janet Kelly

B: **hùwa moo moujòod**
he's not here

B: **hìya moo moujòodah**
she's not here

B: **min yatakàlam lou samàнt?**
who is calling, please?

B: **intàzar shwàya lou samàнt**
just a moment, please

B: **mùmkin àakhuz risàalah?**
can I take a message?

A: **thank you, I'll ring back later**
shùkran, sa-atàsil fee maa bà'ad

A: **thank you, can you ask him/her to ring Riyadh 456789?**
shùkran, mùmkin tàтlub mìnhu/mìnha li-yatàsel bee fil-riyàal 456789?

A: **thank you, please say Mr Jones called**
shùkran, qul làhu in as-sàyid Jones itàsal

A: **when will he/she be back?**
àmta sa-yàrja'/sa-tàrja'?

B: **shùkran, mà'as-salàamah**
thank you, goodbye

If the going gets tough:

A or B:

I'm sorry, I can't understand what you're saying
àna àasif walàkin maa àfнam shoo taqòol

wait a moment
intàzar shwàya

please ring later
itàsil fee maa bà'ad lou samàнt

please speak English
itakàlam inglèezee lou samàнt

please speak more slowly
ta kàlam Àla màhalak lou samàHt

can you say that again, please?
mùmkin taqòolha màrah thaanèeyah lou samàHt?

television tiliviziyòon

telex tilèex

temperature (*fever*) Haràarah
he has a temperature Andàhu Haràarah

terms (*of contract*) shuròoт

terrible faझèeA

than min
it's better than this one hìya àHsan min hàazee

thank you shùkran
thank you very much alf shukr
(*literally: a thousand thanks*)
no thank you la shùkran

that (*with masculine nouns*) zàalik
(*with feminine nouns*) tilk
that man zàalik ar-ràjul
that flight tilk ar-rìHlah
can I have that one? mùmkin àakhuz hàadee?
what is that? shoo hàaza?
that's for you hàaza lak

the al-

THE

To make any singular or plural noun definite, you add **al-** to it as a prefix:

kàlimah	word (or a word)
al-kàlimah	the word
fanàadiq	hotels (or some hotels)
al-fanàadiq	the hotels

If the noun begins with any of these letters: **d, th, t, z, s, sh, D, l** and **n** then the l of the **al-** changes into that letter as well. For example:

sayàarah	car (or a car)
as-sayàarah	the car
тaa'iràat	aircraft (or some aircraft)
aт-тaa'iràat	the aircraft

You will notice that **al-** is never stressed.

theatre màsraH

THEFT *see* STEALING

their -hum

> There are no possessive adjectives as such in Arabic; instead a suffix is added to the noun. In the case of 'their' you add **-hum** to a word ending in a consonant and **-t-hum** to a word ending in a vowel or **-ah** (in which case the **h** is dropped):

> **house**
> bayt

> **their house**
> bàyt-hum

> **company**
> shìrkah

> **their company**
> shìrkatum

> If you use an adjective with 'their' then the word **al-** must be added to the adjective. For example:

> **their new house**
> bàyt-hum al-jadèed

theirs màalhum

> **is this bag theirs? – no, it belongs to that woman**
> hal tìlka ash-shànTah màalhum? – la, hìya maal tìlka as-sayìdah

them

> This can be either the direct object of a sentence as in 'we saw them'. Or it can be the indirect object as in 'I gave them a cheque'.
> When 'them' is used as the direct object you simply add the suffix **-hum** to the verb and move the stress in the word to the preceding syllable. It is important to remember that the plural **-hum** is used only when 'them' is used to refer to people. In other cases 'them' is translated by the non-human plural (which is in fact the feminine singular) **-ha**.

> **we saw them**
> (*people*) ìHna shufnàhum
> (*things*) ìHna shufnàha

> **he put them** (*the children*) **in the car**
> waDà'hum fees-sayàarah

> **he put them** (*the boxes*) **in the car**
> waDà'ha fees-sayàarah

I asked them to my house
da'òutuhum ìla bàytee

When 'them' is used as an indirect object, referring to people, you again use the suffix **-hum** but in this case it is usually associated with a preposition. It is never stressed. If 'them' is not human, use the feminine singular **-ha**:

	HUMAN	NON-HUMAN
from them	mìnhum	mìnha
to them	làhum	làha
on them	Alàyhum	Alàyha
at their place	Àndhum	--

Remember we often omit 'to' in English when we really mean 'to them':

I gave them my passport
aATàytu làhum jawàaz sàfaree

this ticket is for them
hàazee at-tazkàrah làhum

we ate our dinner at their place
akàlna Ashàa'na Àndhum

then (*after that*) wa ba'adàyn
(*at that time*) fee zàalik al-wàqt

there hunàak
there is ... fee ...
there are ... fee ...
is there ...? fee ...?
are there ...? fee ...?

these hàadool

they
If 'they' refers to humans the pronoun is **hum** and it takes a plural verb. If 'they' refers to non-humans the pronoun is **hìya** and it takes a singular verb.

hum: if you want to say 'they are. . .' you just say **'hum ...'**:

they are teachers
hum mudarisòon
(*literally: they teachers*)

they are directors
hum mudaràa
(*literally: they directors*)

they are very ill
hum marDàa jìdan

The pronoun **hum** can be omitted if it is clear from the context and the form of the verb that 'they' is the understood subject of a verb:

>**they arrived yesterday**
>(hum) wàsaloo ams

hom: if you want to say 'they are. . .' you just say 'hom . . .':

>**where are they?**
>wayn hom?
>(*literally: where they?*)

>**they are in the car**
>hom fees-sayàarah
>(*literally: they in the car*)

You can never omit **hom** when it means 'they' or the whole idea of plurality may be lost since it is followed by a singular verb.

thick (*not thin*) samèek

thin raqèeq

thing shay [(*pl*) ashyàa]

think fàkar [yufàkir]
>**what do you think?** shoo rà'yak?
>**I think so** a'aTàqid
>**I don't think so** laa a'aTàqid
>**we'll have to think about it** làazim nufàkir fèeha

thirsty ATshàan
>**I'm very thirsty** àna ATshàan jìdan

this (*with masculine nouns*) hàaza
>(*with feminine nouns*) hàazee
>**this man** hàaza ar-ràjul
>**this visit** hàazee az-ziyàarah
>**can I have this one?** mùmkin àakhuz hàaza?
>**is this yours?** hal hàaza màalak?
>**this is Mr MacDonald** (*introducing him*) hàaza hùwa as-sàyid MacDonald

those hàadool

throat Hànjarah

through An Tarèeq
>**through Riyadh** An Tarèeq ar-riyàaD

Thursday youm al-khamèes

ticket tazkàrah [(*pl*) tazàakir]

tie (*clothing*) kravàtah
  (*borrowed from the French* cravate)

TIES

In the Arab world outside Saudi Arabia and the Gulf States you will find that professionals prefer to wear a short-sleeved shirt and a tie to work. Jackets really are out of the question except for the most formal meetings – perhaps with ministers or senior diplomats – on account of the sweltering heat prevailing for most of the day in most places. In Saudi Arabia and the Gulf States the local businessmen and professionals will wear the traditional Arab robes (*see* CLOTHING) and there is certainly no room for a tie there! Professionals from other Arab countries working in those countries will still wear the shirt-and-tie they are used to at home.

    Western travellers who are travelling on professional or commercial business – as opposed to tourism – should stick to the short-sleeved shirt and tie look when they are at work. This is acceptable everywhere and you can always put the tie in your pocket if you find you are over-dressed. Ties are not generally worn socially except in a formal or quasi-formal setting such as an embassy party, business dinner or day out with senior business partners. You cannot go wrong if you wear a short-sleeved shirt and carry a tie about with you during your visit.

tight (*schedule*) muHàdad
  (*fit, clothes*) Dàyiq

tights sharàab Harèemee

time waqt
  there's not much time maa fee waqt bàaqee
  we've plenty of time Andàna mùdah Tawèelah
  last time al-màrah al-akhèerah
  next time al-màrah al-jàayah
  what's the time? as-sàa'ah kaam?

TIME

Telling the time in Arabic is fairly simple. First here are the hours:

    the time is . . .
    as-sàa'ah . . .

one o'clock	al-wàaHidah
two o'clock	ath-thaanèeyah
three o'clock	ath-thàalithah

four o'clock	ar-ràabi'ah
five o'clock	al-khàamisah
six o'clock	as-sàadisah
seven o'clock	as-sàabi'ah
eight o'clock	ath-thamàaneeyah
nine o'clock	at-tàasi'ah
ten o'clock	al-Aasharah
eleven o'clock	al-Hàadeeyat Aashahrah
twelve o'clock	ath-thaanèeyat Aasharah

The twenty-four hour clock is very rarely used at all.

To say **at six o'clock** you just say:

as-sàa'ah as-sàadisah

To make it **half past six** you just add:

. . . wa nùsf

To make it **quarter past six** you add:

. . . wa rùbA

And to say **quarter to six** you add:

. . . ìlaa rùbA

If you have to say **X minutes past an hour**, you say:

(the hour) wa X daqèeqah

X minutes before the hour is:

(the hour) ìlaa X daqèeqah

These are the most important time words:

hour	sàa'ah
half an hour	nusf as-sàa'ah
quarter of an hour	rùbA as-sàa'ah
minute	daqèeqah
second	thàaneeyah

Let's look at these in practice:

the time is half past three
as-sàa'ah ath-thàalithah wa nùsf

it's five to eight
as-sàa'ah ath-thamaanèeyah ìlaa khàmar daqà'iq

it is a quarter past two
as-sàa'ah ath-thaanèeyah wa rùbA

the time is twenty-nine minutes past nine exactly
as-sàa'ah at-tàasi'ah wa tìs'ah wa Ashrèen daqèeqah bi-dìqah

timetable (*for travel*) jàdwal

tip (*to waiter etc.*) baqshèesh

TIPPING

In the Gulf States tipping is not widely practised, but elsewhere in the Arab world a tip of 10–15 per cent is normal for services such as hairdressing and guided tours. In restaurants you will usually find that a service charge of between 10 and 15 per cent has already been added to the bill and if so a further tip is unneccessary. In cafés where a service charge is not normally shown on the bill leave a tip of 10–15 per cent on the table. This is important, since the waiters are often paid very little by the proprietor of the establishment and rely on tips for their livelihood. Just pay this with the bill. Porters, bellhops and cloakroom or lavatory attendants should get the equivalent of 50p–£1.00 depending on the sort of establishment you are in.

It is not necessary to tip taxi-drivers, although you may wish to reward particularly helpful cabbies with 10 per cent. Do not force tips on people – respect a polite refusal or you may cause offence. Having said all that, it is a good idea to have some loose change handy when you go out (*see* MONEY) so that you have something to give the small (and not so small) boys who helpfully tag along and show you the way to the mosque, bazaar or hotel when you are looking bewildered. You will have to use your commonsense – you will be able to tell from their eyes whether you have underdone it (or overdone it for that matter!).

If you are using the services of a water seller or a fruit-juice seller or a shoe-shine boy in the street, do not ask how much it costs. You will probably get the aggrieved reply:

ma làka?
what is it to you?

since it will always be so cheap you could not baulk at the price whatever it was.

tired ta'abàan
I'm tired (*said by man*) àna ta'abàan
(*said by woman*) àna ta'abàanah

tissues warq klèenix

TISSUES

In the Gulf States tissues have completely replaced the handkerchief, which can still be seen further West, although there too it is becoming obsolete.

to ìla
   to London ìla lòndon
   to Hotel . . . please ìla fùnduq . . . lou samàнt

toast (*drinking*) nakhb

TOASTS
Alcohol is never drunk in Saudi Arabia and it is barely tolerated in many other Arab countries. However, if you are drinking alcohol, the customary toast is:

   fee siнàtak
   to your health

It is said when the drinks have been served and the drinkers are about to pick up their glass. When the proposer of the toast has said it, you then lift your glass and say the toast yourself.

tobacco tibgh

today al-yòum

toe ùsbuA al-qàdam

together mà'an
   can we pay together? mùmkin nàdfa' ma' bà'aD?
   (Note that **mùmkin nàdfa' mà'an** would mean 'can we pay at the same time')

toilet tooaalèet تواليت
   can I use your toilet? mùmkin astà'amil at-tooaalèet?

toilet paper warq tooaalèet

TOILETS
You will come across both the Western-style toilet and the Arab-style ones. Arab-style toilets have no bowl – just a hole in the porcelain floor and two strategically placed raised foot-supports. They are supposed to be more hygienic than Western-style toilets since the body does not come into contact with them, but this is a matter of personal opinion. Even in public lavatories, of which there are few, you will find both types. The main problem that users of the Arab-style toilet may encounter is that, when they are flushed, water tends to cover the whole toilet, including the foot-supports and anything that may have been put on the floor for safety.

It is wisest to plan to leave the cubicle at the exact moment of flushing.

On no account consider relieving yourself behind a tree, wall or car unless the alternative is likely to be even more embarrassing. This is simply not done. Cafés always have a toilet, often of dubious quality, though you should buy at least a soft drink first.

tomorrow bùkrah
    tomorrow morning bùkrah fees-sabàaн
    tomorrow evening bùkrah feel-masàa
    the day after tomorrow bà'ad bùkrah

ton тun

tongue lisàan

tonight al-yòum bil-làyl

too (*excessively*) jìdan
    (*There is no Arabic word for 'too' – you just say* **jìdan**, *which means 'very'*)
    (*also*) àyдan
    it's too expensive hùwa ghàalee jìdan
    me too wa àna àyдan

tooth sin [(*pl*) asnàan]

toothache wàja' al-asnàan

toothbrush fùrshat asnàan

toothpaste ma'ajòon asnàan

top (*of box etc.*) ghiтàa'

total (*noun*) majmòoA

tour (*noun*) jòulah

tourist sàa'iн

towel fòoтah

town madèenah [(*pl*) mùdun]
    in town feel-madèenah

tradition taqaalèed

TRADITION
Tradition is very important to the Arab way of life and change for change's sake is incomprehensible to the Arab way of looking at the world. Traditional habits die hard and are still firmly embedded in society in the Gulf States and in rural areas everywhere. For example: people prefer to eat sitting

round a big tray on the floor rather than sitting up at a table, often not using any cutlery at all, just their right hand, to help themselves; tradition ensures that the young show respect and obedience towards the old; when a young man gets married it is still the custom everywhere for him to give his wife a dowry, and it is common for him to live in the family home with his new wife; in many countries tradition maintains the separation of the sexes quite rigidly and it is fair to say that this is one of the main characteristics of Arab society.

Since the Second World War, and especially since the quadrupling of oil prices in 1973, many Arab states have industrialized very quickly and what a Western traveller sees when he visits the Arab world is a society which has many of the outward symbols of industrial development – the sort of development which took two hundred years to happen in the West – such as banks, factories and a transport infrastructure. These have all appeared within a generation in the Arab world. It is not at all surprising that underneath all this modern development, the traditional system of social organization and political structure have continued relatively unaltered in many places. Indeed it could be argued that it is the strength of Arab tradition that has enabled the Arab world successfully to face up to the challenge and change of recent times without disintegrating entirely, and it is remarkable how cohesive Arab society has proved to be in the face of Western influence. Any profound trends in society take generations to show themselves fully, and it is quite unrealistic, and would be quite wrong, to expect Arab society simply to abandon its traditional ways of behaving over a period of forty years just because of events elsewhere in the world – which often have unpleasant and unresolved side-effects such as loneliness, despair and the search for ever more stimulation – all afflictions which are refreshingly absent from traditional Arab society.

train qiTàar

translate tàrjam [yutàrjim]
   could you translate? mùmkin tutàrjim?

translation tàrjamah

translator mutàrjim

travel sàafar [yusàafir]
  This is the origin of our word 'safari'.

travel agency wikàalat safareeyàat وكالة السفر

traveller's cheque sheek siyàaнee

tray seenèeyah

tree shàjarah [(*pl*) shàjar]

tremendous Dukhm

trial period fìtrah Àla sabèel at-tàjribah

tribe qabèelah

trousers banталòon

true saнèeн
  that's true hàaza saнèeн
  that's not true hàaza moo saнèeн

trust sàdaq [yusàdiq]
  we must trust each other làazim nusàdiq ba'aDìna

try нàawal [yuнàawil]
  we'll try sa-nuнàawil

Tuesday youm ath-thulathàa'

Tunisia tòonis

Tunisian toonèesee

turnover (*of business*) нajm al-a'amàal

twice maratàyn

typewriter aàlah kàatibah

typist kàatebah

tyre iтàar [(*pl*) itaaràat]

U

ugly qabèeн

umbrella shamsèeyah

under (*spatially*) таНт
   (*less than*) àqal min

understand fàham [yàfham]
   I don't understand maa àfham
   I understand àfham

United Arab Emirates al-amaràat al-ʌrabèeyah al-mutàнidah

United States al-wilaayàat al-mutàнidah

الولايات المتحدة

until Hàtta

unusual ghayr ʌadee

up fouq
   this way up (*package*) hàazee al-wàajihah lil-à'alaa
   sales are up al-mabee'àat irtàfa'at

urgent ʌajil

us

This can be either the direct object of a sentence as in 'they saw us' or it can be the indirect object as in 'she gave us her address'.

When it is the direct object you simply add the suffix **-na** to the verb and move the stress in the verb to the preceding syllable. For example:

   they saw us
   hum shaafòona

   he asked us to the conference
   da'àna lil-mu'atàmar

   he pulled us into the shop!
   hùwa saнàbna ìlad-dukàan!

When 'us' is used as an indirect object, you again use the suffix **-na** but in this case it is usually associated with a preposition. It is never stressed.

for us	làna
on us	ʌlàyna
from us	mìnna

Don't forget that we often omit the 'to' in English
when we really mean 'to us':

> **they gave us the money**
> aATòo làna al-fulòos

use istàkhdam [yastàkhdim]
   can I use . . .? mùmkin astàkhdim . . .?

useful mufèed

usually Àadatan

V

valid (*passport, contract*) saàree al-maf'òol

valuable (*adjective*) qàyim

vegetarian nabàatee

veil Hijàab

VERBS

Under each verb in this book we have given two forms. For example:

> **think** fàkar [yufàkir]
> **write** kàtab [yàktub]

The first form is the masculine singular past tense from which you can easily form any part of the past tense (*see* PAST TENSE).

The second form is the masculine singular future tense from which you can again easily form any part of the present or future tense (*see* PRESENT TENSE, FUTURE TENSE). In dictionaries you will normally find both forms given and from these you can devise any part of the verb you wish.

In English we use the infinitive of a verb, 'to think' or 'to write', as the general description of that verb, but Arabic uses the masculine singular past tense as the main way of mentioning a verb in general terms. This is, of course the first one given under each verb in this book. An Arabic teacher would say 'today we're going to look at the verb kàtab'.

very jìdan
  very good koowàyis jìdan
  very tired ta'abàan jìdan
  I like it very much ajabàanee jìdan
  (*Note that the Arabic word for 'very' comes after the word it refers to and not in front of it as in English*)

village qàryah

visa vìza

visit (*noun*) ziyàarah
  we enjoyed our visit istimtà'ana bi-ziyaaràtna

VISITING

When you visit someone at their home it is normal to take a little present for their children – perhaps a toy or a box of sweets. If you are unsure whether there are any children then take a bunch of flowers for the lady of the house. The best you can do for your bachelor friends is a box of chocolates, since every Arab has a secret passion for very sweet things (*see* FOOD).

If the visit is scheduled to last more than an hour or two you will usually find that a meal has been timed to coincide with it. Even on a short visit you will be expected to eat something, and rather than refuse outright, it is best to settle for a little something at the outset, probably a piece of cake, and then both you and your host will feel that convention has been honoured.

When you arrive at an Arab's house you will be greeted by:

àhlan wa sàhlan
welcome

to which you conventionally reply:

àhlan wa sàhlan beek
welcome to you

When you are about to leave you smile and say:

shùkran jazèelan
thank you very much

to which you will hear the response:

ma' as-salàamah, bàytee bàytak
goodbye, my home is your home
See also GUESTS

voice sout

VOICE

The one thing that you will notice about an Arab's voice when he is talking to anybody is that he will tend to use the tone and volume of his voice as much as the actual words to express his feelings and get his message across. Raising the voice does not necessarily signal anger as it tends to do in the West but is merely intended to demonstrate the strength of feeling, good or bad, in the speaker's mind.

W

wait (*verb*) intàzar [yantàzir]
   don't wait for me laa tantazìrnee
   wait for me intazìrnee
   I'll wait for you sa-antàzirak
   I'm waiting for someone (*e.g. said to waiter*) àna muntàzir sadèeqee

waiter jarsòon (*borrowed from the French* garçon)
   waiter! ya jarsòon!

waitress naàdilah
   waitress! ya àanisah!

Wales waylz

walk (*verb*) màsha [yàmshee]
   let's walk there khalìna nàmshee hunàak

wall Hàa'iT [(*pl*) HeeTàan]

wallet màHfazah

want aràad [yurèed]
   that's not what I want hàaza moo ìlli ureedàhu
   I want . . . urèed . . .
   I don't want to maa urèed
   what do you want? shoo turèed?
   he wants . . . yurèed . . .

warm (*climate, day, person*) daàfee

was *see* **be**

wash (*verb*) ghàsal [yàghsil]

watch (*wristwatch*) sàa'ah

water maay مياه
   a glass of water, please koobàayat maay lou samàHt

water-pipe (*to smoke*) nargèelah

way: which is the way to . . .? minwayn aт-тarèeq ìla . . .?

we ìHna
   Note that the verb 'to be' is implied (in the present tense). For example:
      we are accountants
      ìHna muHaasibòon

(*literally: we accountants*)

we are her parents
ìHna waalidàyha
(*literally: we her parents*)

we are teachers at the law college
ìHna mudarisòon fee kulèeyat al-Huqòoq

The pronoun **ìHna** can be omitted if it is clear from the context and the form of the verb that 'we' is the intended subject of a verb.

we arrived yesterday
(ìHna) wasàlna ams

weak (*material*) Da'èef

weather al-jòu
what weather! ya làhu min jou!

WEATHER

The Arab world lies astride the Tropic of Cancer and at sea-level is subject to sub-tropical climatic conditions: hot and dry in the summer and warm and humid in the winter with no extreme cold. Obviously in the mountains the temperature does get colder and in the desert, which covers a large part of the Arab world, night-time temperatures can often fall below freezing just before dawn. In the desert rain is notable by its almost complete absence. Desert covers the Arabian Peninsula except for the south-western corner and most of the hinterland of the North African Arab states of Egypt, Libya, Tunisia, Algeria and Morocco. Elsewhere the rains tend to fall between October and April except in the Gulf, which often gets its rainfall in July and August as it catches the western edge of the monsoon weather-system which normally develops over the Asian sub-continent at that time.

For those British and North European travellers who are used to six months of winter followed by six months of bad weather the Arab world provides refreshing straightforwardness. During the summer high-pressure systems set in over the whole region (except the Gulf) for months and anti-cyclonic dry and hot weather is guaranteed. The Egyptian Western Desert is alleged to be the sunniest place on earth!

When the rains do arrive in winter or spring, it

rains torrentially and there is often flooding, as the
dry land cannot absorb it quickly enough.

Lightweight suits for men and dresses for women
are the sensibl things to pack all the year round,
although a hat and raincoat should be taken just in
case in winter and spring. You can leave your gloves
and ear-muffs behind unless you are planning a hike
through the mountains of Algeria, Morocco or Syria
in winter, where you will even find snow.

In summer always pack a hat of some sort even if
you never normally wear one, since ten unprotected
minutes under the desert sun in summer can lay you
up for days if you are unused to it.

wedding 'urs

WEDDINGS
A wedding is a very big event in the Arab world and
a person's wedding is undoubtedly the most important and frequently the happiest day of their life. It
is celebrated differently in different Arab countries
and the scale of the festivities depends on the wealth
of the families concerned. The man usually gives
the woman a dowry and arranges a big feast where
lambs and even camels are eaten. All the friends and
relatives of the happy couple are invited and if they
are wealthy the feast may last several days.

In Egypt, where segregation of the sexes is less
rigorously enforced than elsewhere, the bride and
groom sit together at the feast and everyone joins in
one grand shindig, singing, dancing and eating. In
the Gulf States and other more traditional countries
there are two parties: one hosted by the bride for the
women and one hosted by the groom for the men.
Either way a good time is had by all!

Wednesday youm al-arba'àa

week usbòoA [(*pl*) asaabèeA]
    next week feel-usbòoA al-jàay
    last week feel-usbòoA al-màaDee
    for two weeks li-mùdat usboo'àyn
    three weeks ago min thalàatha asaabèeA

weekend nihàayat al-usbòoA
    at the weekend fee nihàayat al-usbòoA

WEEKENDS
The concept of 'weekend' as it is known in the West
is unknown in the Arab world. The weekly break in

government departments, schools and universities
occurs on Thursday afternoon and the whole of
Friday, which is the Muslim day of rest and prayer.
You will, however, often find shops and traders open
on both these days. Our Western idea of at least two
days together as a break-week when you can do
things apart from your work or business is not at all
widespread in the Arab world and you would be wise
to leave your idea of a weekly holiday behind you.
The only time things do come to a halt in business
in the Arab world is during Ramadan (*see*
RAMADAN).The shutdown during that period is so
complete that it is often a waste of time even trying
to do business there and you are advised to avoid
planning any business trips to Arab countries during
that month unless you have been specifically invited.

weight wazn

welcome: you're welcome laa shùkran Àlal-wàajib
   thank you for your very warm welcome shùkran Àla
   muqaabalàtak al-karèemah

well (*in health*) jàyid
   not well (*in health*) marèeD
   I'm very well thank you (*as response*) al-Hàmdulìllah
   bi-khàyr
   things are going well al-Hàal màashee tamàam
   you speak English extremely well ànta tatakàlam
   inglèezee mùmtaz jìdan

were *see* **be**

west al-ghàrb
   in the West feel-ghàrb

Western-style Tarèeqah al-gharbèeyah

wet mablòol

what? shoo?
   what is that? shoo hàaza?

wheel Àjalah

when? àmta?
   when does it start? àmta tàbda'?

where? wayn?
   where is it? (*masculine object*) wàynhu
   (*feminine object*) wàynha

which: which one? ay wàaHid?
   which company? ay shìrkah

whisky wèeskee

white àbyaD

who? min?

why? laysh?
   why not? laysh laa?

wide ArèeD

wife zòujah

WIFE

In many Arab countries, especially the Gulf States and in rural areas everywhere, it is expected that once a girl has completed her education she will get married and have children. Thereafter her place is firmly in the home. In those societies very few wives go out to work. In the large cities and away from the Arabian Peninsula wives are now starting to go out to work but this is mainly out of economic necessity, to boost the family income, rather than a sign of great social emancipation. *See* MARRIAGE.

will *see* FUTURE TENSE

wind (*noun*) reeH

window shubàak
   a window seat, please kùrsee janb ash-shubàak lou samàHt

wine nabèez

winter shitàa
   in the winter feesh-shitàa

with
When 'with' means in the company of, among or beside you use **ma'**. When it means by use of or containing you use **bi-**. Compare the following examples:

   you are with friends here
   ànta ma' asdiqàa hùna

   he is in England with my father
   hùwa fee ingiltìra ma' àbee

   I want a cup of tea with sugar
   urèed finjàan shay bi-sùkar

   I cut my finger with a knife
   jaràHtu usbà'ee bi-sikèen

without bidòon
  without sugar bidòon sùkar

woman imrà'ah

WOMEN

The emancipation of women which has spread slowly through the Western world since the French Revolution and proceeded apace in the twentieth century has yet to make much headway in the Arab world. Arab society is totally male-dominated and yet within it women can rise occasionally to pre-eminent positions in the cultural, medical and academic fields. A Westerner will best understand the status of women in the Arab world by comparing it with that of women in Victorian Britain – it is much the same. A woman's place is in the home, but exceptionally there is a way upward as a teacher, artist, writer or as a nurse or even doctor. However, there is always a ceiling to the possibilities for achievement for women in the Arab world and this will probably remain the case while the three places it matters are still closed to them: government, the mosque and the army. Incidentally, we Westerners cannot be too smug about our societies when they are given this analysis!

wood (*material*) khàshab

wool soof

word kàlimah
  what is the word for . . .? shoo al-kàlimah li . . .?

WORD ORDER

The normal word order in Arabic is the same as in English: subject + verb + object + any adverbs:

  the man went to the shop
  ar-ràjul raaH ìla ad-dukàan

  the manager signed the letter quickly
  al-mudèer wàqa' Àla ar-risàalah sarèe'an

work (*noun*) shughl
  it's a lot of work hàazee shughlàanah kabèerah
  it's not working (*machine etc.*) al-màakinah aTlàanah

worry: don't worry laa tanzà'ij

worse àswa

write kàtab [yàktub]
  could you write it down? mùmkin taktùbha?

writing: Arabic writing al-kitaàbah al-ʌrabèeyah

WRITING

Until the 1880s there wasn't a single printing press in the Arab world. Until very recently, really after the Second World War, the Arabic word meant the Arabic hand-written word. A whole study and art of calligraphy had developed since 650 A D and until the eighteenth century Arabic was much more clearly and uniformly written than any of the European languages.

Nowadays much Arabic is printed on printing presses and so, of course, runs along a straight line which robs it of much of its beauty. Arab printers have been aware of this and usually put the headlines in a special typeface (*see* ARABIC), or get them hand-written, so the Arabic letters can flow above and below the line making a different, original version of each sentence each time.

With the onset of Western-style advertising in the Arab world advertising agencies have tried to devise new eye-catching ways of printing Arabic script and, with all the lines and dots, have much more promising material to work with than the twenty-six Roman letters which Western designers have at their disposal. Nevertheless most Arabs consider Arabic a language which looks at its best when it is hand-written and would agree that the carefully and beautifully hand-written ornate manuscripts of the past 1,300 years cannot be remotely matched by the printing-presses of the past thirty or so years (*see also* ALPHABET, ARABIC).

wrong ghalΤàan

Y

yawn (*verb*) tathàa'ab [yatathàa'ab]

year sànah

YEARS

Arab businesses and governments use the Western solar calendar, which is reckoned in years A D just as in the West. There is a Muslim lunar calendar which uses its own system of twelve months (*see* CALENDAR) and each lunar year has only 354 days. This Muslim calendar dates from 622 A D, the date of the flight of Muhammad from Mecca to Medina, and these years, of course, pass more quickly in relation to the solar years. 1988-9 A D corresponds to 1409 A H (anno hegirae).

Here some basic phrases:

last year
fees-sànah al-maaDèeyah

this year
fee hàazee as-sànah

next year
fees-sànah al-jàayah

yellow àsfar

Yemen: North Yemen al-yàman ash-shimàalee
South Yemen al-yàman al-janòobee

Yemeni yàmanee

yes àywa

YES

Instead of saying just **àywa**, which can sound a bit abrupt to an Arab, you will often hear **insha'àllah**, which means literally 'if God wills'. For example, if someone at the dinner table offers you some meat and asks:

hal turèed laнm?
do you want some meat?

you could only answer:

àywa
yes

However if someone asks you:

hal bi-taròoн ìla wàsaт al-madìnah?
are you going to the city centre?

then to reply:

insha'àllah
yes (if God wills)

is most appropriate and better than **àywa**, which would sound rather bald.

yesterday ams

yet: not yet lìssa bà'ad

YOU

Arabic is unusual in that you have to use a different form of the pronoun 'you' depending on the sex of the person you are speaking to:

ànta	means 'you' when addressed to a man
ànti	means 'you' when addressed to a woman
àntum	means 'you' when addressed to a plural number of men, women or a combination of the two

Note that the verb 'to be' is implied (in the present tense). For example:

you (*fem.*) **are only a tourist**
ànti saa'ìнah fàqaт
(*literally: you only tourist*)

you're the boss!
ànta ar-ra'èes
(*literally: you the boss*)

you are my friends
àntum asdiqàa'ee

The pronouns **ànta/ànti/àntum** may often be omitted, since it is usually clear from the context that 'you' is the intended subject of the verb.

when did you arrive?
àmta wasàlta?

young saghèer

your
There are no possessive adjectives in Arabic, instead a suffix is added to the word. In the case of 'your' there are three options to be considered depending

on whether the word 'your' is used to refer to a man, a woman or a group of either or both.

If it refers to a man, you add -ak to a word ending in a consonant and -tak to a word ending in a vowel or -ah (in which case the h is dropped). For example:

hotel
fùnduq

your hotel
fùnduqak

company
shìrkah

your company
shìrkatum

John, your children are in the water!
ya John, awlàadak feel-maay!

If it refers to a woman, you add -ik to a word ending in a consonant and -tik to a word ending in a vowel or -ah (in which case the h is dropped). For example:

Josephine, your mother is arriving on the next plane
ya Josephine, ùmik satàsil ʌlaт-тaa'ìrah al-jàayah

If it refers to a group of either or both, you add -kum to a word ending in a consonant and -tkum to a word ending in a vowel or -ah (in which case the h is dropped). For example:

where are your manners, children!
wayn aadàabkum ya awlàad!

If you use an adjective with 'your' then the adjective must have the prefix al- attached to it:

your heavy box (*said to a man*)
sundòoqak ath-thaqèel

your heavy box (*said to a woman*)
sundòoqik ath-thaqèel

yours (*belonging to a man*) màalak
  (*belonging to a woman*) màalik
  (*belonging to a group*) màalkum

is this suitcase yours, madam?
hal hàazee ash-shànтah màalik, ya sàyidah?

is this suitcase yours, my friends?
hal hàazee ash-shànтah màalkum, ya asdiqàa'ee?

is this David's ticket? – no, it's yours!
hal hàazee at-tazkàrah mal David? – la, hìya màalak!

Z

zero sifr
zip sòostah

NOTES